KOREAN FOLK-TALES

Oxford Myths and Legends in paperback

*

Korean Folk-tales

Retold
by
JAMES RIORDAN

OXFORD UNIVERSITY PRESS

OXFORD NEW YORK TORONTO

Note

The front cover picture on this edition is of Hwang Won
Jong, a pavilion in the royal palace compound, while the
back picture shows Shim Chung on the lotus blossom. Inside
the book, the chapter opening script is the original name for
the Korean alphabet, and the motif at the end of the chapters
is the Yin Yang symbol.

Oxford University Press, Walton Street, Oxford OX2 6DP

Oxford New York Toronto
Delhi Bombay Calcutta Madras Karachi
Kuala Lumpur Singapore Hong Kong Tokyo
Nairobi Dar es Salaam Cape Town
Melbourne Auckland Madrid

and associated companies in
Berlin Ibadan

Oxford is a trade mark of Oxford University Press

A CIP catalogue record for this book is available
from the British Library

ISBN 0 19 274160 8

Printed in Great Britain

To Kang Shin-Pyo and John MacAloon
who first introduced me to the
Land of the Morning Calm

CONTENTS

Dan-Gun, First Emperor of Korea

HWAN-IN, the Celestial Emperor, had a bold, wise son called Hwan-Ung; one day the lad asked his father for an earthly land to rule.

'You may choose the land yourself, my son,' the Emperor said. 'But judge well, for you will create the first human life in your new kingdom.'

As he looked down upon the earth, the young prince's gaze fell upon the green hills of a beautiful peninsula between two great seas.

'There, that is the land I want,' he told his father.

The Emperor granted his son's wish and sent him down to earth to found the Korean nation. He was accompanied by three thousand servants to help him rule the land, and three powerful ministers: Pung-Beg, U-Sa and Un-Sa —Lord Wind, Lord Rain, and Lord Cloud.

1

They were to govern health and sickness, harvest and season, good and evil.

The noble Hwan-Ung set up his home in a sandalwood tree on Tebeg Mountains, now Myohyang-San, in the north, and there established the Sacred City.

Shortly after, the Heavenly Prince summoned a tiger and a bear who lived in a nearby cave.

'I have chosen you to become the first humans,' he told them. 'Here, take these twenty garlic bulbs and this mugwort plant; eat them and remain deep in your cave for a hundred days. When you emerge into the daylight you will be man and woman.'

So the tiger and the bear ate the garlic and mugwort plant and went to their cave. The bear was patient, enduring the dark, damp cave without food for a hundred days; but the tiger could not sit alone for long with no food. It ran away into the hills.

As the bear emerged from its long vigil into the sunlight, it suddenly changed into a beautiful young woman. The bear-woman was overjoyed with her new form. She went straight to the sacred sandalwood tree to thank the Heavenly Prince.

'But where is the tiger?' asked the Prince.

'Oh, he ran away before the hundred days,' she said.

'That's a pity,' he replied with a frown, 'for he was to be your husband and father of your children. Never mind, you will be empress of this land and bear a son with no father; he shall be known as Dan-Gun, the Sandalwood Emperor.'

And so it was that Prince Dan-Gun was born some four thousand three hundred years ago. When he was grown to manhood he became the first human emperor of the land. He built his capital at Pyongyang and gave his kingdom the name Chosun—Land of the Morning Calm. Later in life he moved his capital to Mount Asadal, now Mount Guwol in Hwang-He Province. Today it is the site of a holy shrine called Sam-Song or the Three Saints: Hwan-In the Celestial Emperor, Hwan-Ung the Heavenly Prince, and Dan-Gun the first human emperor of Korea.

Folk say that when Dan-Gun died he became a San-Sin or Mountain God. He is never forgotten by the grateful people of Korea.

Blindman's Daughter
Shim Chung

IN THE Land of the Morning Calm, there once
lived a poor blindman Shim-Pongsa and his
beloved daughter Shim Chung. When
Chung's mother died in childbirth, Shim-Pongsa
had to take Chung from house to house in search
of mothers' milk to keep her alive. And as she
grew older, her father took her with him through
the village, begging for food. So Chung became
well known and loved by all the neighbourhood.
She was a kind and hard-working girl, devoted to
her father.

When she was twelve a nobleman's wife
offered her work as a maid; this pleased Chung, for
she could work all day in the big house and take a
little food home to her father at twilight.

One day, however, she was late returning
home; since he was anxious for her safety, Shim-
Pongsa went out to meet his daughter. Feeling his
way along the path with a stick, Shim-Pongsa

came to a narrow bridge across the stream; but in his haste, he slipped and fell into the water.

'Help, help, save me,' he cried, splashing in the water.

He was lucky. A passing monk heard his shouts and ran to pull him out. The monk took Shim-Pongsa home and, on learning that he was blind, told him how he could regain his sight.

'You should take three hundred sacks of rice to Buddha's temple and you will see what you will see.'

In his excitement old Shim-Pongsa promised he would do just that. At last he would see his daughter!

But when the monk had departed, the blindman began to regret his foolish promise. Where would he obtain one sackful of rice, let alone three hundred?

Finally Chung came home. She was late because of a party at the nobleman's house. But she had brought her father some rice cakes. When he only picked at the food and hung his head in silence, she realized something was wrong.

'What is the matter, Father? Are you unwell?' she asked.

'No, no,' the old man sighed.

Yet he was eager to shed the burden lying heavily upon his heart, and he soon told her all about his misadventure, the monk, and the foolish promise.

5

'How could I promise Buddha three hundred sacks of rice?' he muttered. 'But a promise to Buddha must be met. I have to find the rice somehow.'

Little Chung prayed each day to the Heavenly Spirit to help her father find the rice; she would do anything to make her father's dream come true.

One day soon after, Chung overheard her mistress telling the nobleman a story of some sailors; they were searching for a young maiden to sacrifice to the Sea Dragon, so that they could sail safely through the stormy China Seas. They would pay any price.

Chung's heart leapt for joy.

Learning where she could find the sailors, she set out for an inn in a nearby port. When she found their captain, she told him, 'I am ready to be your sacrifice. My price is three hundred sackfuls of rice.'

The captain and his crew listened to her story and were moved by her willingness to die to restore her father's sight. At first the captain refused; but she persisted and finally a deal was struck: three hundred sacks of rice for the maiden's life.

'Our ship sets sail at the next full moon,' the captain said on parting.

As the sailors loaded up oxen wagons with rice to take to Buddha's temple, Chung ran home to tell her father the wonderful news.

'Father, Father,' she cried on entering the house, 'the rice is on its way to the temple. All three hundred sackfuls. Soon you will be able to see.'

'But where on earth did you get so much rice?' asked her father in astonishment.

Chung had never told her father a lie in all her life. Yet now she feared to tell the terrible truth; so she bit her lip and stammered, 'Oh, the n-n-nobleman's wife wants to adopt me. Sh-sh-she gave me the rice in payment. I'll be moving to the big house at the next full moon.'

The blindman laughed for joy, more for his daughter than for himself.

'I'm so pleased for you,' he said. 'Now you'll always have enough to eat.'

With the passing of the days and the waning of the moon, poor Chung began to tremble with fear. She did not want to die, but most of all she did not want to leave her father. Who would look after him when she was gone?

There was still much to do before she had to leave, and she would work late into the night washing and darning her father's clothes, stitching his old horsehair hat, replacing the rice paper over door and window frames, mending the bedding. At long last, all was done.

On the eve of her departure, she sat beside her father, gazing sadly at his sleeping form. Tears rolled down her pallid cheeks as she pondered his fate: he would have no one to care for him.

'I wish the dawn would never come,' she sobbed. 'I wish the cock would never crow. I wish the moon would never be full . . .'

All too soon the sun sailed over the mountain, the cock began to crow, and she heard the sailors at the door.

'Just give me a moment to cook my father's breakfast for the last time,' she begged. 'He does not yet know my fate.'

The sailors looked at her grief-stricken face and nodded their assent.

Closing the door softly, she woke her father and made ready the tastiest meal he had ever eaten.

'Father, eat your fill,' she said. 'I want to make you happy.'

Of course, Shim-Pongsa could not see her tear-filled eyes or shining cheeks. He ate hungrily and looked up in pleasure.

'My, this food is good,' he said. 'It surely is not my birthday, is it?'

Chung remained silent, biting her lip.

After a while, her father said, 'Do you know, I had a dream last night. In the dream you were riding in a carriage drawn by four snow-white horses. That must be a good omen. Since you will be living in the nobleman's house, my dream may well come true some day.'

Chung burst into tears, for she knew the dream foretold her death. It was her body being carried to heaven in the horse-drawn carriage that her father had seen.

'What's wrong, my child?' he exclaimed. 'You must not cry, you'll be happy with the nobleman. And if you are happy, I am happy.'

Running to the corner of the room, Chung knelt before the family altar to bid farewell to her ancestors and ask their pardon for abandoning her father. Bowing twice, she then returned to her father and threw herself at his feet. She could not leave without telling him the truth.

'Oh, Father, please forgive me. I did not tell you the truth. I am not going to the nobleman's house. I sold myself for three hundred sackfuls of rice as sacrifice to the Sea Dragon. Now it is time for me to go.'

Her father was horrified.

'No, no, it can't be true,' he cried. 'My sight is no good to me if I cannot see you. My life is worthless without you. Don't leave me.'

Too late. The sailors were at the door again.

Father and daughter hugged each other, weeping on each other's shoulder. Abruptly, Chung tore herself away and, with her father's cries ringing in her ears, she ran from the house after the sailors.

They were soon on board and, the moon being full, made good headway upon the high seas. For several days the sea was calm, the waves gently lapping at the ship's sides, the sea breeze gently blowing its sails. It was the lull before the storm.

As they rounded the island of Indangsu, they ran into a storm that made the sea seethe and rage, tossing the ship about like a fly in a boiling cauldron. It seemed the lurching ship would break apart at any moment.

'It's the Sea Dragon,' the sailors yelled. 'He'll drown us all unless we send him a sacrifice.'

All eyes turned to Chung.

She knew what she had to do.

Climbing into the bow of the ship, she shut her eyes tight and jumped into the angry sea.

'Farewell, Father,' she cried before the waves closed above her head.

In an instant the sea was calm. Staring wistfully at the spot where she had drowned, the sailors sighed and then sailed on.

Yet Chung did not drown.

As her body sank into the watery depths, a sea nymph took pity on her. Catching the lifeless form in her arms, the nymph swiftly gave her gills to breathe through underwater, like a fish. Then, accompanied by a school of tuna fish, she carried her down, down, down to the ocean floor where they entered the Sea Dragon's palace. And there the sea nymph put the lifeless girl upon a bed before the Sea Dragon.

The fierce old Sea Dragon's heart was softened by the innocent young beauty before him. Instead of killing her there and then, he decided to make her his daughter.

When Chung at last opened her eyes and gazed about her, the splendid sights helped her overcome her fear. The palace hall was so magnificent, decorated by glittering pearls and pink and orange coral; nymphs were dancing to music plucked on silvery strings. A tray of seafood dishes stood before her. And everyone was so kind and happy she soon lost her fear.

Yet, with thoughts of her father weighing heavily upon her, she could not bring herself to eat or smile. Of course, she offered thanks to the Sea Dragon for sparing her life and making her a nymph princess. And she told him of her life.

As the days went by her sombre mood never changed, and finally the Sea Dragon relented. He had dearly wished her to stay within his ocean realm, but it was clearly best to send her back to her father. So he had her placed inside a giant red lotus blossom which floated up to the surface of the sea. It was there that the nymph who had first found her removed the gills, so that she could breathe air again.

The lotus blossom floated upon the calm sea for several hours until, by chance, a fishing boat came into view and the fisherman spotted the unusual flower. It was truly a gift fit for a king. So he brought the flower on board and took it to the emperor.

The emperor was delighted with the gift. Imagine his amazement, however, when the lotus blossom slowly opened to reveal Chung fast asleep inside. The young emperor fell in love at first sight and was determined to make her his wife.

So Chung became empress. She was happy with her new life and proved a good and generous empress to the people. But, now and then, her eyes would fill with tears at the thought of her poor father. One day her husband saw the tears and learned her story. After thinking for a while, he told her his plan.

'We will reward all the blind people in the land with a special gift. Should your father be alive he is bound to come here for his prize.'

The proclamation was read in every town and village of the realm. And in next to no time, blind men began arriving at the palace to claim their prize. Each day Chung anxiously searched the faces as they passed her. Without success.

On the very last day, when she was losing hope, she suddenly spotted a gaunt, shabby figure shuffling through the palace gates. Wild with joy, she rushed through the throng and threw her arms about the old man's neck.

'Father, Father,' she cried. 'It's me, your daughter Shim Chung.'

Old Shim could not believe his ears. He

opened wide his long-shut eyes and, lo and behold, the darkness cleared. 'I can see! I can see!' he shouted. 'My daughter is alive.'

Chung's sacrifice had not been in vain.

Both the sighted and the blind who witnessed this miracle wept tears of joy, and retold the story for the remainder of their lives.

Shim lived out his days in contentment with his daughter in the royal palace. As for Empress Chung, she had many children, and grandchildren to follow. And you can be sure that her daughters and granddaughters learned of the bold, wise ways of Korean women from Shim Chung.

Weaver and Herdsman
Chik-Nyo and Kyun-Woo

LONG, LONG AGO in a land beyond the stars there lived a fair princess, the only daughter of the Heavenly Ruler. Because she loved weaving, she was known as Chik-Nyo, the Weaving Maid. Each day she would weave delicate patterns on rugs and clothes and tablecloths.

The emperor was very proud of his clever daughter and often watched in silence as she worked upon her loom. There is no greater happiness than to have a daughter who works hard.

One day, as he looked on, he was surprised to see the face of a young man appear upon her cloth. At first he was cross, but he soon realized that his daughter was a girl no more; she had become a pretty young woman and it was only natural that, now and then, her thoughts should turn to men.

Chik-Nyo was so ashamed: her fingers had betrayed her thoughts. She had intended to weave a pattern of flowers for her father.

Now she wept with shame.

'Do not cry, Chik-Nyo,' her father said. 'I'll find a good match for you and make you happy.'

So the Heavenly Ruler summoned all his wise men and commanded them to find the perfect husband for his daughter. After consulting for several days, a choice was made.

'We have found the ideal husband for the princess,' announced the wisest of the wise. 'He is a handsome prince from the neighbouring realm. Since he likes herding cattle, he is known as Kyun-Woo, the Herdsman. What could be better: weaver and herdsman?'

An envoy was duly despatched to the neighbouring realm to arrange the wedding. And, as fortune would have it, the prince's father was delighted with the proposition. He too thought it the perfect match and his star-gazers pronounced the omens right for the perfect pair.

A wedding date was set and the realms began preparing for the great event. As was the custom, both sets of parents advised the children on their roles as man and wife.

'Be true to each other, work hard, and always obey your parents. Then you will find perfect happiness.'

At last the happy day arrived and Chik-Nyo married Kyun-Woo. There was not a more contented and devoted couple anywhere in the universe. They were so in love that they wished only to be together, hold hands, and gaze into each other's eyes. They played games all day long, sometimes lying in each other's arms, counting the stars. Chik-Nyo's loom grew rusty for want of use. Kyun-Woo's cattle grew skinny for lack of food and soon ceased to give milk.

As the weeks passed into months, word went from mouth to mouth and finally came to Chik-Nyo's father who hated laziness. On hearing that the newly-weds were neglecting their duties, he sent for them at once.

When they came before him, he flew into a rage, shouting, 'Your parents instructed you to work hard and obey them. But you have disobeyed. All you do is play the whole day through and count the stars, run about the meadows and pick flowers. You set a bad example to our people and so must be punished.

'Since you both loved work when you were apart, it is because you are together that you are now idle. I shall therefore punish you by making you live apart. You, Chik-Nyo, shall weave in the west of the realm, while you, Kyun-Woo, shall take your cattle and abide in the east.'

The loving pair were overcome by grief.

'Oh, Father, please do not part us,' cried Chik-Nyo, tears streaming down her cheeks. 'I could not live without my dear husband. I'll do anything you say—only let us be together.'

'Oh, Your Majesty,' exclaimed Kyun-Woo.

'Please forgive us. We are so in love that we have neglected all else. But we'll make up for it. Just see how hard we'll work from now on.'

The Heavenly Ruler was unmoved by their pleas. He sent Chik-Nyo to a distant realm far to the west; there she would spend her time weaving. As for Kyun-Woo, he was despatched to a remote land in the east, along with all his cattle.

Chik-Nyo and Kyun-Woo wept for so many days and nights that the Heavenly Ruler finally relented. He sent word to his daughter and her husband that they could meet once a year beside the Silvery Stream. It was to be on Chilsok, the seventh day of the seventh moon.

From then on Chik-Nyo spent the days sitting at her loom and gazing towards the eastern heaven where her beloved lived. Kyun-Woo, too, could not keep his mind upon his work. As he tended his cows, his thoughts were ever on his dear Chik-Nyo and his gaze was turned to the western heaven where she lived.

A year went by. Chilsok arrived—the one night in the year when they could meet.

With fast-beating hearts, each set out on the long journey across the skies to the Silvery Stream. As they caught sight of each other in the distance, each cried out happily:

'Chik-Nyo!'

'Kyun-Woo!'

Repeating the other's name, they began to

run towards each other. Suddenly, however, they stopped, on opposite banks of the Silvery Stream. It was so wide they could barely see each other upon the distant shore. There was no bridge, nor boat.

The two lovers stared in desperation across the water.

They cried and cried in their anguish. And their tears fell to earth as rain, flooding the land below and threatening the lives of birds and beasts whose homes would soon be washed away.

The birds and the animals called a council.

'We must do something before we all drown,' grumbled the big black bear.

'But we cannot reach the land beyond the stars,' growled the tiger.

'I know,' barked the fox. 'Let's ask the wise old owl. He'll know what to do.'

So they went to the owl. All the birds and beasts of the earth gathered beneath the bough on which sat the wise old owl.

The owl related the sad story of the two 'heavenly beings', the cause of their plight.

'The only way to stem the flood of tears is to help them cross the Silvery Stream,' he concluded gravely.

A gloomy silence descended upon the animals. Then, all at once, a voice chirped up:

'I know,' said the magpie. 'Why don't the

magpies and crows make a bridge for them to cross over the stream?'

It was worth a try.

The sky turned black as all the crows and magpies upon the earth flew up into the sky. Up and up they soared until they reached the heavens; on and on they flew until they came to the Silvery Stream. Then, with their wings spread wide, they formed a bridge across its glistening waters.

When the two lovers next gazed through tear-filled eyes, they stared and stared. For there was a bridge where none had been before. In a trice, Chik-Nyo ran lightly across the wing-span bridge and threw herself into her husband's arms. All night long they held each other tight in a fond embrace. Yet as dawn began to break, they had to part once more and Chik-Nyo tripped sadly across the bridge. Shedding a few last tears, they each made their lonely way to their east–west homes.

From that time on, there are always light drops of rain in the early morning. And on the seventh day of the seventh moon you will never see a crow or magpie. If you do see them on the following day, mark well their loss of feathers: for they lost them as Chik-Nyo stepped lightly upon their heads while crossing the Silvery Stream, so that she could be with her husband for one night of the year.

*   *   *

If you look up at the sky on 7 July (the seventh day of the seventh moon) you can see two bright stars (Chik-Nyo and Kyun-Woo) in early evening on either side of the Silvery Stream (the Milky Way).

Son-Nyo the Nymph and the Woodcutter

THERE ONCE lived a woodcutter with his mother at the foot of Diamond Mountain in northern Gangwon Province. He was a hard-working lad, but so poor there was not a girl in the village who would marry him. So he looked after his aged mother and each day went up the mountainside to cut wood. The villagers would say of him, 'Though the sun may not shine every day, there's always the ring of the woodman's axe upon the mountainside.'

One day, as he was gathering fallen branches amid the tall pines and firs, he suddenly heard a crashing and pounding in the trees; looking up, he saw a deer plunging wildly down the slope towards him. Blood smeared its mottled coat from an arrow wound in its side.

'Woodman, please save me,' it cried. 'A hunter is after me and my strength is nearly spent. Can you hide me?'

'You poor creature,' he said. 'Quick, hide beneath these pine branches.'

Just as he finished concealing the animal, a burly hunter came riding up, shouting roughly, 'Hey you, did you see a deer run this way?'

'Yes, I did,' he answered truly. Then he added, 'It ran straight past and down towards the valley below.'

Without a word, the hunter took up the chase and disappeared down the mountainside.

As the deer emerged from its hiding place, it thanked the man.

'You saved my life. Now I want to do you a service. You see, I am really the daughter of San-Sin, the Mountain God. For your kindness I will grant you a wish.'

'My mother and I may be poor, but we are content,' said the woodcutter. 'We have all we need.'

But then he thought how it would please his mother to see grandchildren before she died.

'There is one thing though,' he shyly said. 'Sometimes I wish I had a wife to love and bring me children; that would make my mother happy.'

'So be it,' said the deer. 'On the fifteenth day of the month, when the moon is full, climb to the top of Diamond Mountain; there you will find a lake of crystal-clear water where the seven nymphs, the *son-nyo*, come to bathe. They will undress and leave their robes upon the shore. Watch closely and choose one for your wife: then swiftly snatch up her dress and hide it. For without her silken dress she cannot fly.

'When they have finished bathing, six will fly off to the heavens, the seventh will remain upon the shore. That is your chance: go and claim her for your wife. But mark my words well. Do not return her silken dress until she has borne you four children.'

With these words, the deer bounded away up the mountain.

The woodcutter could hardly wait until the fifteenth day of the month. As that day drew to a close and the full moon cast its light upon the mountain slopes, he set out up the track until he reached the mountain top. And there, in a circle of trees and bushes, he came upon the most beautiful lake. Streams of crystal water flowed into it, some tumbling over rocks in waterfalls; the lake's waters glistened in the moonlight, reflecting the dark green trees and gaunt grey cliffs about. Small wonder the old folk say, 'Speak not of beauty until you've seen Diamond Mountain.'

The woodcutter hid among the bushes and waited with fast-beating heart. Soon seven lovely maidens flew down from the skies to the lakeside; there they cast off their silken robes and plunged happily into the cool waters of the lake where they splashed and swam to their hearts' content. Each had long raven–black hair and skin the colour of moonlight.

Scarcely able to tear his gaze away, the woodcutter remembered the deer's words: he stole out from his hiding place, quickly snatched up a silken robe, put it inside his jacket and concealed himself again behind the bush. Out of sight, he watched the naked nymphs at their play. At long last, as day began to dawn, the maidens came out to dress. They had to return home before the closing of the Heavenly Gates.

One by one, the lovely maidens flew up into the sky, leaving the poor unfortunate girl with no clothes upon the shore. She searched high and low for her robe before sinking to the ground in tears.

It was then that the woodcutter appeared.

'Don't cry, Son-Nyo,' he said kindly. 'I'll look after you, come home with me and be my wife.'

She begged him to return her robe, and he was moved by her sobbing pleas; yet he stood firm, following the deer's advice. Putting his jacket about her trembling form, he led her by the hand down the mountainside to his home. Although his mother greeted the maid warmly, she would not be comforted at all.

Poor girl. She lay down in the corner and wept the whole night through. Likewise the next day too, and through the week. But there came a time when her tears dried up and there was nothing for it but to make the best of her new mortal life. The woodman was kind and gentle, if a mite unpolished in his ways. He gave her enough to eat and taught her all a mortal wife should know.

The weeks grew into months and life took its course: within a year a son was born. And in the passing of time another entered the mortal world. After each child's birth, she begged her husband to return her robe.

'Can you not see proof of my love in our child?' she would ask. 'You may rest content: show me my robe, I'll not betray you.'

But each time he was mindful of the deer's warning. Although he was moved by her pleas, he was afraid of losing her and his children. So each time he replied sternly, 'No, I do not trust you.'

Truth to tell, she thought of nothing but her home in the skies, of the heavenly garden with its twinkling star-flowers and sweet fragrance, of her sisters, her parents, and her friends.

When a third child was born, she prepared tempting dishes and strong rice wine for her husband. And when he had eaten and drunk deeply, she kissed him lovingly. With tears rolling down her cheeks, she begged him one more time.

'Dearest husband, will you not show me my robe in honour of our third child's birth? I just wish to see and touch it again. If you love me, you will surely do this to please me.'

The woodman's heart was full of love and sorrow for his wife, and he showed her the robe he had long kept hidden. He quite forgot the deer's warning.

'Oh, how smooth and fine the silk is,' his wife exclaimed. 'Let me put it on to show our children.'

He felt shame at not trusting her all these years; and he let her take the robe from his trembling hands. When she had put it on she called the two older children.

'Come, my darlings, and see your mother's lovely robe.'

When they were all assembled, she quickly gathered up the children, ran outside with them and flew up to the skies, a child under each arm, the third between her legs.

'Come back, come back,' cried the grief-stricken husband.

His wife's voice drifted to him on the breeze.

'Dear husband, though I love you well, I must return to my own home. Farewell, you will never again see me or our children.'

The poor woodcutter was inconsolable. Even his mother could not comfort him. He sat and wept through the days and nights and wandered far into the mountains crying out his grief.

One day, not long after, the selfsame deer appeared out of the trees.

'You did not heed my warning,' it said, 'and now you pay the price.'

'I am so sorry, San-Sin's Daughter,' he said, holding his head in his hands. 'Is there nothing I can do?'

'There is one way, but it will not be easy,' the deer said. 'Listen well this time. Since you stole the robe, the seven nymphs no longer come to the starry lake to bathe. But on the fifteenth day of the month, when the moon is full, they lower a wooden bucket on a rope to take the crystal water.

'If you climb into that bucket, they will pull you up, unsuspecting. That is how you may see your family again.'

With those words, the deer was gone as if it had never been.

The woodcutter could hardly contain his impatience until the fifteenth day of the month. At dusk he was at the lakeside, eagerly searching the skies; finally, at midnight, a large bucket on a thick rope descended from the heavens into the middle of the lake. As swiftly as he could, he dived into the cold waters and swam to the bucket before it was out of reach; scrambling into it and grasping the rope firmly, he felt himself rising through the air, up and up and up, through clouds of mist, until he came into a land of blue skies and golden earth.

How astonished the seven nymphs were to find a man instead of water in the bucket. Yet his wife let out a cry of joy, begging the others not to send him tumbling back to earth.

'Let us take him to Father,' she cried. 'Let the Celestial Ruler decide his fate.'

So it was decided. And their father, seeing his daughter's radiant face, agreed to let the human stay with his family.

Life was quite different in the heavenly realm. The woodcutter had no work or worries; he could play with his children all day long; he was dressed in fine clothes and he ate the most delicious food. All the while, he had his lovely wife beside him. Even so, now and then his thoughts wandered back to earth: how was his poor mother faring all alone? She must miss him. No one would care for her in her declining years.

Finally, he made up his mind to pay a visit to his mother.

'Dear wife,' he said one day, 'I have to see my mother one last time before she dies. It is my duty as a son.'

She begged him not to go, for she did not want to be parted from him again.

'No, husband, if you return to earth,' she said, 'you will never see your family again.'

But he persisted until, at last, she went to her father for advice. On returning to her husband, she said, 'There is a way. A winged horse will fly you down to earth to see your mother. But whatever you do, never leave the horse's back; should your feet touch the ground, the horse will fly straight back without you. And you will remain on earth until your dying day.'

He assured her that he would do exactly as she said: he would never allow his feet to touch the ground. With that he mounted the winged horse and, in the twinkling of a star, he was beside his mother's humble home.

How overjoyed she was to see him after all this time. They each told of their lives since last they met, the son explaining why he could not dismount from the magic horse.

She did not press him. However, as they were parting, she said, 'I have prepared some pumpkin soup; I know it is your favourite. Come in and eat a bowl before you leave.'

'No, no, I must not leave my horse,' he said.

Yet not wishing to disappoint her, he asked her to fetch it to him. So she brought a bowl of hot soup, holding it up to him.

As he took it from her, however, the hot bowl burned his hands and he spilled some soup on to the horse's back.

With a loud neigh of pain, the horse reared up on to its hind legs, hurling him to the ground. He could only watch in helpless grief as the horse flew up into the sky and disappeared beyond the clouds.

He had lost his dear children and beloved wife: never again would he see them. Each day he would stand beside his home, gazing up through tear-filled eyes, searching the heavens for his wife and children. He pined away in his loneliness and died of a broken heart soon afterwards.

Folk say that on the day he died a red-combed cockerel flew up to the rooftop, stretched its neck towards the sky and crowed loud and long, as if its heart would break. It was really the spirit of the poor woodcutter, who every day since then cries his loud lament, searching for his family in the sky.

The Snail Woman

LONG, LONG AGO, there was a young man who lived all alone in a straw-thatched hut. His parents were dead and he had no brothers or sisters for company.

One day as he was working in the paddy field he set to recounting his misfortune.

'Here I am nearing thirty; no woman will wed a man as poor as me. Why do I plant rice when there's no one to share it with?'

'Share it with me,' came a woman's voice.

He looked about him, yet saw nobody.

'I must be hearing things,' he said, continuing with his work. But just in case, he said aloud, 'I've no one to share my life with.'

'Share it with me,' came a woman's voice again.

'Who spoke there?' he shouted, glancing all around.

Again he saw nobody.

A third time he spoke up, 'I've no one to share my home with.'

This time he listened keenly for the reply.

'Share it with me.'

How odd. The sweet voice seemed to come from beneath his feet. Yet all he could see was a snail, half buried in the mud. Just for luck he picked it up and dropped it into his pocket. He heard no more voices, so he cast the woman's words out of his mind.

When he arrived home at dusk, he washed, ate his meagre supper and went to bed. Next morning, when he awoke, he was surprised to smell food cooking. As he glanced up, he saw a tableful of tasty dishes and a bowl of steaming rice. Not waiting to discover who had prepared such a splendid meal, he sat down and ate his fill.

Then he toiled all day in the paddy field. As he came home at dusk he once again found the table set with a delicious feast, more tasty than he had ever known. Hungrily he sat down and finished the meal, thinking how fine it would be to have a wife who cooked so well.

'I must find out who this cook can be,' he thought to himself.

Instead of going to bed, therefore, he hid beneath the table concealed by the tablecloth, and kept watch. In the early hours of the morning, he was amazed to see a beautiful young woman emerging from the snail's shell; when she was fully grown, she stepped from the shell, cooked the breakfast, washed the floor, darned his clothes and then shrank back into the snail shell.

Soon after he crept out from under the table and ate his breakfast before going off to work. So it continued for three more days. He could not help thinking how wonderful it would be to have her for his wife; so he made up his mind to try to catch her unawares.

On the third morning, he ate his breakfast as normal and made as if to go to work. Hiding behind the hut, he waited until she had risen from her shell before rushing into the room. Poor girl, she hastily tried to squeeze herself back into the shell. Too late, he seized her hand and held her tight.

'Dear Snail Woman,' he implored her, 'please stay with me and be my wife.'

She was silent for a while, a rosy blush upon her flushed cheeks. Finally, she looked up and murmured, 'I will be your wife. But you should know that I am the daughter of the Dragon King. I was unjustly punished by my father and turned into a snail for seven moons; now my time is up and I can decide my own fate. I shall therefore share my life with you, as I promised in the paddy field.'

So the two lived together happily as man and wife, he planting rice for the two of them, she cooking food and keeping house.

One day, however, a wealthy magistrate rode past the house and saw the beautiful woman in the yard.

'How can such a lovely woman be wed to a rice planter?' he thought. 'She is fit only to be the wife of a man such as I.'

And he set to thinking how he might take her from the poor man. Ordering the husband to be brought before him, he gave this command, 'We shall pit our strength against each other. All my wealth for your wife. We'll see which of us can cut down trees faster on yonder hill.'

The poor man would not trade his wife for anything. But she whispered in his ear, 'Take this note tied to my ring and cast it into the sea. My father, the Dragon King, will come to your aid. Trust me.'

He did as she said.

Just as he was about to throw the ring into the sea, however, the waters parted, uncovering a sandy path leading down into the depths. He walked along the trail until he reached the ocean bed; on he went until he arrived at the Dragon King's underwater palace.

As soon as he had read his daughter's note, the Dragon King gave his son-in-law a leather bag and sent him home.

As the day of the contest dawned, the magistrate set hundreds of his men to chop down the trees. But the poor man, following the

Dragon King's instructions, slit open his leather bag and out poured a host of tiny men wielding axes; they set about them, chop, chop, chop, and in next to no time the hill was shorn of trees. Of course, the poor man was declared the winner.

Yet the magistrate was not yet done.

'Let us pit our wits together one more time,' he growled. 'We will race each other across the river on horseback.'

Once more the snail wife sent her husband with a message to the Dragon King. And this time he returned on an old nag that looked as if it would fall down dead at any moment. And yet, when the contest started, the scrawny nag ploughed through the waters like a knife through oil, leaving the magistrate and his noble steed floundering in its wake.

The magistrate was furious.

'Give me one last chance,' he said. 'This time we'll race our boats across this broad river.'

Once more the poor man went to the Dragon King, and this time came back with a tiny skiff hardly big enough for him to fit inside. The magistrate, sitting comfortably in his large boat, smiled smugly to himself. This time he was bound to win.

Yet as the race began, the tiny skiff shot ahead like an arrow from a bow; it crossed the raging river in no time at all. So angry was the magistrate that he jumped up and down on the deck of his boat in a rage, tipping it right over. He was swallowed up in a swirling wave and was never seen again.

As for the poor man, he was perfectly content with his lovely wife and simple home. He gave all the magistrate's wealth to the poor, and got on with planting rice in his paddy field.

The Distant Journey

CHUN-KYU WAS poor and alone. His parents were dead. His humble hut was so empty you could wave a stick without striking anything.

He often pondered on finding fortune and happiness, and one day he met an old man who told him this:

'Somewhere, far away, at the very top of Diamond Mountain, lives an aged sorcerer who can set you on the road to fortune and happiness. The way is long and hard: ninety-three days from here.'

Chun-Kyu's mind was made up. He was determined to go in search of his fortune. No matter how hard the journey—through rivers and valleys, over mountains and hills, down steep cliffs and gullies; there were dense forests full of fierce animals ready to pounce on the unwary traveller. His friends and neighbours tried to dissuade him from the perilous journey; others shook their heads, saying, 'If you were born to fortune, you'd find ginseng in your own backyard. No sorcerer can help you.'

But Chun-Kyu would not listen. All he said was, 'I've nothing to lose since I've nothing to own. I've just one knapsack to bear my worldly possessions upon my back. So off I shall go.'

Besides, the young man had learned a secret: if you go to the sorcerer with a song, the path will not seem so long. And though he was poor, he was rich in song. So, strapping his knapsack to his back, he set off on his distant journey with a song:

> Sing out, you merry song,
> Sing out.
> I am travelling through
> My dear Chosun.
> My strong boots
> Will carry me through
> Long days and nights,
> As I journey through
> My dear Chosun.

Many a tall mountain, many forests and plains, many a stream and valley were left behind as Chun-Kyu tirelessly journeyed on without a rest, all the while singing his songs:

> No fields can compare
> With those of my native land.

Play on, my reed pipe, play on;
We've come many hundred *li*.
The path to fortune
Is not far now.

Truth to tell, Chun-Kyu had not yet covered
half the distance to the aged sorcerer. Yet, all of a
sudden, as he made his way through a dense
thicket, he noticed a light flickering in the forest
gloom. Quickening his pace, he soon came to a
woodland glade; and there in the light of a fire
he saw a lone white cottage, exactly like his
own.

'Who could be living in such a forsaken
place?' he was wondering when, all at once, the
door opened and there stood a maiden of radiant
beauty. Her skin was as smooth as velvet, her eyes
sparkled like the stars, her shoes shone like
diamonds and her multicoloured robe of pure
silk shimmered in the flickering light.

Captivated by her beauty, he bowed low to
the ground, murmuring, 'Fair maiden, my journey
has led me to your door; and now the dark night
has veiled my onward path. Dare I beg a night's
rest? Pray, pardon my tattered clothes and rough
appearance.'

The fair maid bowed and said, 'What you
bear in your soul is more important than what you
wear on your back. And you cannot carry a night's
rest with you: all travellers, rich or poor, on

horseback or on foot, have to rest sometime. Since you are at my door, do come in; my home is big enough for two.'

When Chun-Kyu entered the cottage he unstrapped the knapsack from his shoulders with a sigh of relief.

'Tell me, dear mistress,' said Chun-Kyu, 'what am I to call you?'

'I am Poon Kot-San,' she said. 'Since I am unwed I bear my own name. And you, dear guest, what is your name and whither are you bound?'

'Dear Kot-San,' he replied, 'my name is Chun-Kyu and I am on my way to an aged sorcerer who lives far from here, at the very summit of Kymgansan, the Diamond Mountain. I go there to seek my fortune.'

'Oh, do ask him a question for me too,' she said. 'I wish to know my destiny; who am I to wed?'

'Be sure, dear Kot-San,' he replied, 'I shall do my best to gain an answer to your question.'

They bowed timidly to one another; the mistress went to the fire in the glade and soon returned with a dish of peppered radish and a bowl of warm noodles. Having served the wayfarer some supper, she threw a few handfuls of fresh-mown hay upon the mattress for him to sleep.

Next morning very early, Chun-Kyu rose and thanked Kot-San for her hospitality and set off once more upon his distant quest.

He was long upon his journey, treading untrodden forest paths, forcing a way through dense brambles and ferns. Finally, he saw daylight filtering through the trees; the forest came to an end as a broad plain stretched ahead. Beyond the plain glimmered a blue strip of water on the far side of which he could see wooded hills. Cutting a staff at the forest edge, he struck up a new song:

> My staff,
> You go before
> To lead the way.
> Be my guide
> All the way to the
> Top of Diamond Mountain.
> As I go I sing
> Kot-San, Kot-San;
> Will I see you again?
> Who knows? Who knows?

When Chun-Kyu had crossed the broad plain, he came to the river, foaming and swirling on its course. No raft could take him across those waters; anyway, all he had was his trusty staff. Squatting at the water's edge, he set to thinking, 'How am I to cross this raging river? Who will aid me?'

And he sighed. The more he sighed, the louder the river seemed to be sighing with him. Then, all at once, huge waves rose up and out of the crest of a towering wave there appeared an enormous fire-breathing dragon, with red bulging eyes and flames bursting from its jaws and nostrils.

'Fear not, bold fellow,' roared the dragon, striking the waters with its long tail and cleaving them to the river bed. 'All that is born of the river is not evil; I will take you across to the other side. Only tell me first: whither are you bound? What is your quest?'

'I am going to the top of Kymgansan where an aged sorcerer dwells,' said Chun-Kyu. 'I shall ask him how to gain fortune and happiness. That sorcerer can help anyone who lives an honest life.'

'Can he help me, do you think?' asked the dragon.

'If you are fair and honest,' replied Chun-Kyu. 'Tell me your need and I will surely ask.'

'I am tired of living in water,' said the dragon. 'How I would love to fly up to the skies and look down on the earth. Perhaps the aged sorcerer can help me?'

'I will ask,' promised Chun-Kyu.

Hardly had he recovered from the dragon's ear-splitting roar than he found himself deposited upon the distant riverbank. On he went, singing at the top of his voice. He went up hill and down dale, through forest and plain, across river and lake until he had covered four and a half thousand *li*. He had been on the road for full ninety days and still the Mountain was not in sight.

As he was starting the ninety-first day, however, he spotted a little cottage at the foot of a hill. When he came closer an old man and woman emerged to welcome him. He told them of his quest and asked if there was anything he could do for them.

'We have lived to a venerable age,' the old man told him, 'and we are quite content. However, we do have one concern: ten years ago we planted a pair of apple trees outside our window. We water and tend them lovingly; yet they give us no fruit. Would you ask the aged sorcerer how to make the trees bear fruit?'

Chun-Kyu promised to convey their request to the sorcerer on Diamond Mountain. After taking a meal with the old pair, he went on his way. Leaning on his trusty staff, he now entered the foothills of a lofty mountain; clambering over sharp crags and steep cliffs, he came at last to the top of the tallest crag and stopped to admire the view. The sun was slowly sinking over the horizon and in its golden-pink rays he suddenly saw a small hut upon the mountain top. A track led upwards and, to his surprise, he saw it was paved with marble flagstones.

After a short rest, Chun-Kyu straightened the knapsack on his back and took a deep breath before stepping out boldly along the marble path leading to the little hut. An old, old man stood waiting for him at the door.

'Ho there, Chun-Kyu,' a voice boomed down the mountainside. 'I have long awaited your arrival: it is now the ninety-third day of your quest. I know well that the path to any noble goal is hard. Yet if you are honest and true you will reach your goal on time and spend the rest of your days in peace and happiness.'

When Chun-Kyu reached the aged sorcerer's home, the wise man said, 'Tell me of your encounters upon the journey; speak truly and leave nothing out.'

'Dear Sorcerer, wisest of the wise,' began Chun-Kyu, 'to you all is visible from the lofty heights of Diamond Mountain. I shall tell you all exactly as it was. I had three encounters upon my journey. The first was at a lonely woodland cottage where I met a maid called Poon Kot-San; hearing of my quest, she asked you to foretell her destiny and whom she would wed.'

The venerable sage bowed his head, his long grey beard touching his knees; after a while he looked up, gazing intently at the young man.

'Chun-Kyu, you have spoken truly,' he murmured. 'You have traversed the entire journey honourably, doing harm to no one and listening to their requests. Tell Kot-San this: let her wed the first man she falls in love with. With him her destiny is bound.'

Chun-Kyu set to memory the sorcerer's

words and straightaway explained the second encounter.

'That dragon needs little for happiness,' said the sage. 'The moment he cures himself of greed, he will be able to fly up to the heavens; tell him that.'

Chun-Kyu described his third encounter.

'Oh, that is easy,' said the sorcerer in response to their request. 'Let them replant both trees on the other side of the garden, and they will gain reward worthy of their toil.'

After recounting his adventures, Chun-Kyu told the sorcerer of his own life. Finally, bowing low to the ground, he asked the question for which he had come:

'Wisest of the wise, my journey to you has been long and hard. Pray, share your wisdom with me and tell me how to find fortune and happiness.'

'Oh-ho, my son,' exclaimed the wise man with a chuckle, 'but that is the simplest thing of all. On your way home fortune will come to you of its own accord, even before you reach your village.'

Chun-Kyu shrugged his shoulders uncomprehendingly; he was disappointed. It seemed he was no wiser than when he had set out. But there was nothing for it. He had come all this way for advice and now he had received it. Thanking the aged sorcerer, he set off on his return journey.

After climbing down the mountainside, he

soon found himself in the valley where the old man and woman lived.

'Will our apple trees bear fruit?' they asked. 'What must we do?'

'You must replant the trees on the other side of the garden,' he told them. 'And you will be rewarded for your lives of honest toil.'

He helped the old pair dig up the trees, for they were heavy and the soil hard. Yet when the roots were lifted out, they found to their astonishment a chest of gold beneath each tree.

'We should never have gained such wealth without you,' they told Chun-Kyu. 'Take one of the chests for yourself; may it bring you happiness in your long life to come.'

Thanking them for their kindness, Chun-Kyu put a chest of gold into his knapsack and went on his way. All the while he leaned on his trusty staff and sang his songs:

> My staff,
> You go before
> To lead the way.
> Fortune is to be found
> Along the way.
> So be my guide
> As I sing of
> Kot-San, Kot-San.
> Will I see her again?
> Who knows? Who knows?

The way home is always shorter than the journey out. And so it was. Next day, Chun-Kyu arrived at the raging river where he had met the dragon. And there it was lying on the sandy strand, its great head resting on its paws, eagerly looking out for Chun-Kyu's return.

At once Chun-Kyu told the dragon of the sage's words.

'You need little enough for happiness. All you must do is cure yourself of greed and you will fly up to the skies.'

'I understand,' roared the dragon, stretching out its tail for the lad to climb upon its back.

A moment later they were on the other shore.

With a sigh, the dragon breathed out two five-sided rubies from its fiery nostrils: one ruby was for Chun-Kyu, the other it kept for itself, saying, 'Let the sorcerer see how I share my fortune equally. That ruby will make all your wishes come true.'

With those words the dragon took a deep breath and flew up into the skies, as happy as a bird.

Chun-Kyu clutched his red ruby as he watched the dragon disappear into the clouds.

'What shall I wish?' he said to himself. 'I know, a flying horse would shorten my journey.'

Hardly had he uttered the words than there appeared a fiery black steed with a silver star upon its forehead and a flaring mane. Its bridle and saddle were of burnished gold which glowed like fire.

'Sit in my saddle, Chun-Kyu,' said the steed. 'I'll take you wherever you wish in the twinkling of an eye.'

Chun-Kyu patted the soft flaring mane and murmured, 'Take me to that dense forest where the lone cottage stands, home of the lovely maiden named Poon Kot-San.'

He leapt into the saddle and flew like a whirlwind over fields and meadows, lakes and strands, until he reached the dense dark forest. He halted his fiery steed right outside the familiar dwelling in the woodland glade. At once the door flew open and the fair Kot-San appeared, gazing fondly at the bold young man.

'How handsome he looks,' she thought, seeing him seated upon his fine black steed.

'Dear Poon Kot-San,' began Chun-Kyu, 'you will find happiness by marrying the man you fall in love with at first sight. There lies your destiny.'

'How fortunate I am,' she gave a joyful cry, 'for you, Chun-Kyu, are the man I fell in love with at first sight. You made the distant journey all by yourself; now we can find happiness together upon our long road.'

And so it was. Many, many years later, so folk say, Chun-Kyu and Kot-San still lived together in peace and happiness to a deep old age. Their distant journey was truly happy since together they lived an honest, hard-working life.

Blindman and the Demons

LONG AGO in Hanyang, capital of the Chosun Kingdom, there lived a blind fortuneteller. He would walk about the streets, tapping his stick and crying out in a wailing voice. Now and again passers-by would ask him what the future had in store: when was the best time to hold weddings and funerals, to move house, or search for lost possessions?

Although he could not see the world about him, he had the power to see evil spirits and ward them off.

One day, as he was on his rounds, he clearly saw a host of demons following a delivery boy carrying a box full of fruit and cakes. The evil spirits were dressed in yellowy orange, greenish blue, and purply red. Suspecting that the spirits were bent on mischief, the blindman followed at a safe distance. Soon after, the boy delivered his box to a wealthy nobleman's house; and the spirits disappeared inside the house.

As the blind fortuneteller waited outside he heard a mournful wailing coming from within the house. Upon enquiring from a servant, he learned that the nobleman's daughter had died a sudden death as if from no cause at all.

'Take me to your master at once,' he told the servant. 'I think I can bring the girl back to life.'

The servant hesitated.

'Quick, we've no time to lose,' urged the blindman.

So he was taken to the grieving father; the blindman explained the cause of the little girl's death.

'You say you can bring my daughter back to life?' asked the nobleman.

'I will try,' he said. 'But first I must drive the evil spirits from her body while it is still warm. I have to work in a room where every nook and cranny is sealed so that the demons cannot escape and do more evil.'

The father was ready to do anything to bring back his beloved daughter; so he had the body taken into a small room and ensured that all the doors and windows were tightly shut, that every crack and cranny was papered over, so that even a needle could not find a gap.

When the blindman was satisfied there was no escape for the demons, he sat beside the girl's body, rocking to and fro and chanting a special spell to drive death out.

Presently, ever-mounting groans and hideous screams filled the room as the spirits cried out in their agony; driven from the girl's body they now flew furiously round the room, seeking an escape from the chanting spell. All the while, the blindman kept up his chant.

However, just as the infernal din was fading, a servant girl could contain her curiosity no longer and made a tiny peephole in one of the papered windows. In a flash, the evil spirits rushed through the hole and out into the world.

In the meantime, the dead girl was coming back to life: she opened her eyes and sat up. Her parents were overjoyed and eternally grateful to the blindman. Yet he, poor soul, sat with head in hands, refusing to accept reward.

'I am done for,' he groaned. 'The demons are bound to take revenge on me; they will hunt me down and kill me.'

Thereupon he left the house and wandered off, tapping his stick and moaning softly to himself.

News of the miracle spread far and wide until, eventually, it reached the emperor himself. Now, he was a wise and cautious man, too accustomed to imposters to be taken in by every miraculous tale he heard. There were too many quacks who cheated innocent people, took their reward and vanished. So he sent for the blind fortuneteller to test his powers for himself.

When the blindman came to the court, the emperor had a dead rat set before him.

'Now tell me,' said the emperor, 'what is before you?'

'It is a rat, Your Majesty,' said the blindman.

The emperor was surprised.

'And how many rats are there?'

'Three,' said the blindman confidently.

'Are you absolutely sure?' asked the emperor with a knowing look to his courtiers.

'Oh yes, there can be no doubt,' replied the blindman.

'Then you are a liar and a cheat,' shouted the emperor crossly. 'Have his head chopped off. I shall make a public example of him so that folk know what happens to imposters.'

The blindman continued to protest as he was dragged out to the Eastern Gate to be beheaded. As his head was being placed upon the block, a courtier who was curious at the blindman's insistence that he saw three rats, cut open the rat. To his astonishment he found two unborn baby rats inside. He rushed to the emperor to show him the three rats, just as the axe was about to fall.

'Good gracious,' exclaimed the emperor. 'The man was right after all. I have made a grave mistake. Halt the execution immediately.'

Now it was the custom in those days for a

guard to hold up a flag from the watchtower in order to signal either the execution or a last-minute reprieve. If he held the flag to the left, it meant the axe should fall; if to the right, the victim was spared.

The signaller now held up the flag to the right.

Yet just at that moment a strong gust of wind blew the flag to the left. No matter how hard the man tried to hold it to the right, the fierce breeze forced the flag to the left.

So the axe came down and the blindman's head was sent spinning from his body.

Straightaway the wind died down as if by magic and mocking laughter echoed round the courtyard. The demons had taken their revenge.

The Fox Girl

THERE WAS once a wealthy man who had a son but no daughter. So badly did he want a daughter that he spent much of his time praying at temples and consulting fortunetellers. Finally, his prayers were answered and a girl was born: she was the apple of her father's eye and could do no wrong.

When she was fifteen years old, the girl went mushrooming on the mountainside and was so engaged in her task that she did not notice the gathering shadows of dusk. Meanwhile, at home, her parents were becoming anxious, and they formed a search-party to comb the hills. However, just as they reached the top of a ridge they spotted the girl through the gloom in the valley below. Her father was much relieved.

'Where have you been, my dear?' asked her father. 'We were so worried for you; a wild beast could have killed you.'

'Forgive me, Father,' she replied. 'I was so tired I fell asleep beneath a bush; when I awoke the sun was already going down.'

The incident was soon forgotten. But a few days later a strange thing happened: one of the master's cows died in the night. Next night another died, then another. The bodies showed no sign of wound or illness. The master was so concerned he ordered the cowherd to keep watch all through the night to catch the culprit.

That night, the man hid behind some hay in a corner of the cowshed and waited patiently. At midnight he was astonished to see the master's daughter creep into the shed and approach a cow. Anxiously he watched her oil her hands and arms with sesame oil; then, to his horror, she slipped her arm into the cow's belly and pulled out its liver. And she ate it.

The poor cow rolled over and died.

In the morning the cowherd went to the master and recounted all he had seen.

The father, who loved his daughter with all his heart, shouted angrily at the man, 'How dare you invent such wicked stories against my daughter. You will pay for these lies.'

And the man was dismissed.

Next night a second cowherd was set to guard the cows. He too hid behind some hay and witnessed the daughter's odd conduct: she oiled her hands and arms, thrust one arm into the cow's belly, pulled out the liver and ate it. And the cow rolled over and died.

Next morning he went to the master and told him the story.

The father still would not believe such tales of his beloved daughter. So the man was dismissed.

A third herdsman spent the night in the cowshed and reported all he had seen. He too was sacked.

Thus it continued: each night a cow died. Then, when no cows were left, the pigs began to die, and then the horses, all of the same mysterious ailment. In the end, all the cowherds, swineherds, and stable boys were dismissed and no one from the village would work for the rich man. All that was left of the once-mighty herd of cattle was a solitary old horse.

Next night, the master sent his only son to solve the mystery. The young man concealed himself behind some hay and kept watch. In the middle of the night he heard footsteps and the barn door opened. It was his sister stealthily entering. In his relief, he was about to cry out to her. Yet something in her look stopped him: her eyes were sly and narrow, her thin lips cruelly curled, her face stony and stern.

He stared in disbelief as she greased her arms and thrust them into the horse's belly, pulling out its liver. With blood dripping from her lips, she then chewed and swallowed the steaming meat.

He dared not breath until she had returned to the house.

At dawn he called his father into the barn and showed him the dead horse.

'Father,' he said grimly, 'you will not like what you hear; but I must tell you the truth. It is my sister. She it is who came in the night and ate the horse's liver.'

His father stared at him with hurt and anger in his eyes. He was silent for a moment, then shouted at his son, 'You must be madly jealous of your sister to make up such tales. No doubt you fell asleep and had a nightmare. Get out of my sight, I don't want you in my house.'

Not knowing where to go, the disconsolate son wandered off into the hills. After several months he came upon an old monk struggling across a mountain stream. Having helped the monk to safety, he was invited to stay the night at a nearby temple. And there he told the story of his sister. The old man nodded sadly.

'Yes, I understand,' he said. 'That night, when your sister was in the hills, she must have been eaten by a fox who took her form, the very likeness of your sister. So it was really the fox who killed the animals.'

'Then I must return at once,' the lad exclaimed, 'and warn my parents.'

'I fear it is too late,' said the old monk. 'Morning is wiser than evening. Set out tomorrow.'

Next morning, the young man was given three small bottles: red, green, and blue.

'Take this horse,' said the monk, 'and use the bottles as I have instructed.'

With that the boy thanked the monk and rode off down the mountain track. It was several days before he arrived home. Once there, he could hardly believe his eyes: the house and yard were overgrown with weeds. And there, in the middle of the yard, was his sister, sitting in the sun, catching lice and worms, and eating them.

'My dear brother,' she cried on seeing him. 'Where have you been all these months? How I've missed you.'

She went to hug and kiss him, but he drew back in alarm.

'Where are Father and Mother?' he asked.

'They lie in their graves,' she replied, giving no explanation for their deaths.

Realizing that she had eaten them too, the young man knew he had to escape before she killed him as well. But how? Suddenly he had an idea.

'Dear Sister, I have come a long way and I'm very hungry,' he said. 'Could you prepare a meal?'

He thought he would escape while she was cooking. But the fox girl was cunning.

'Assuredly, dear Brother. But I shall tie a rope to your leg and the other end to my waist.'

She left him in the yard while she went to prepare some food; every now and then she tugged on the rope to make sure he had not run away. After some time he managed to undo the knot, tie the rope to a gatepost and ride swiftly away on his horse. It was some time before the fox girl realized she had been tricked.

She rushed after him with the speed of a fox and it was not long before she was gaining on him. He glanced back and, to his horror, saw her rapidly catching him up, reaching out her hand to grasp his horse's tail. Recalling the old monk's instructions, he swiftly took the little red bottle from his pocket and threw it behind him.

The bottle instantly burst into a ball of red fire, blocking the fox girl's path. Although the flames singed her hair and clothes, she raced round the fire and was soon overtaking her brother again. This time he threw down the green bottle and straightaway a dense green bush of brambles sprang up, barring her way. Although she was scratched and bleeding from the thorns, she fought her way through and began to catch up with the fleeing brother.

Just as she was about to grab the horse's tail, however, he took out the blue bottle and desperately cast it behind him. This time it formed a mighty blue lake that soon engulfed the fox girl who splashed and thrashed in the water before sinking below the waves.

As the brother watched from the shore, he saw the dead body of the fox float to the surface of the lake. At last he had killed the fox who had taken his sister's form.

The Tiger's Grave

LONG AGO in Zangsu Province a little boy was born into a wealthy family. But when his father died the fortune quickly dwindled and the boy and his mother became so poor they were forced to live in a lowly hut. When the boy had grown to manhood he could not afford to take a wife even though he was honest and hard working. So he was a dutiful son and, as the years passed, cared for his mother as she had cared for him.

One day his ailing mother called him to her, saying, 'Dear son, I have heard there is a good doctor in the village of Unbong; I'm sure he can ease my pain. Please fetch some healing herbs from him.'

The poor lad had no money for medicine, but he could not deny his mother. Borrowing money from his neighbours, therefore, he set off for Unbong on the other side of the mountain. He

61

crossed the ridge by the Zize Pass and reached the village just as the sun was setting.

He explained his mother's illness to the good doctor, paid him for some medicinal herbs and immediately set out for home, carrying the precious medicine in a bag upon his back.

When he came to Zize Pass he peered through the gloom and saw, to his horror, a merchant fighting with a big tiger; the man was grimly hanging on to its tail so that it could not reach him with its jaws. Seeing the young man, the merchant shouted for help. Without hesitation, the young man ran forward.

'Take hold of the tail,' cried the merchant, 'while I fetch my knife and kill the beast.'

At once he dropped his medicine bag on the ground and grabbed the tiger's tail. Once freed from the tiger's clutches, however, the merchant snatched up the medicine bag and made off as fast as his legs could carry him.

Thus, the poor man was cheated of his mother's medicine and his own life too, for his strength would soon give out. Thoughts of his sick mother gave him renewed power and he clung on desperately to the tiger's tail.

But his body gradually grew weak, his knuckles were white and numb, his feet could no longer keep a foothold among the rocks. The tiger's breath was blowing in his face. Finally, with the tiger's triumphant roar ringing in his ears, he collapsed in a dead faint.

Imagine his astonishment when he came to his senses to find not a hair of his body harmed. The tiger was nowhere to be seen. Feeling himself all over, unable to believe his good fortune, he hurried through the Pass and down the mountain-side. Half-way down the track, however, he was surprised to find his medicine bag at the wayside; he was about to pick it up when he noticed with horror the stump of a man's arm alongside; and then, farther off, he saw the bloody remains of a body. He recognized it as that of the merchant who had cheated him. The tiger had evidently torn him to pieces as punishment for his treachery.

When the young man came home he boiled the precious herbs for his mother and in a few days her pain had eased. The story of the son's devotion to his mother and his grim adventure with the tiger soon spread throughout the village and he was much respected as a dutiful son.

One day soon after, he was cutting wood in the hills when he heard gunshots ring out in the trees higher up the slope. In no time at all, a tiger burst into the clearing where he was working and halted, panting before him, its strength clearly spent.

Although he was terrified, the lad looked closely at the beast and recognized that selfsame tiger who had killed the merchant several months before.

'One good turn deserves another,' he thought.

So he hid the tiger beneath a pile of logs and, when the hunters came, he directed them down into the valley below. When all was quiet the tiger emerged from its hiding place,, nodding its great head three times, as if in gratitude, before racing off up the hillside.

One evening soon after, the lad and his mother suddenly heard the heavy tread of a large animal in the yard; when they looked out they were amazed to see the tiger carrying a lovely young girl across its back. Letting her down gently upon the ground, the tiger bounded away into the trees.

The young man picked up the senseless girl and carried her into the house; his mother forced warm soup into her mouth and she slowly recovered, telling them her story.

'I come from Gumsan in the province of Zolla,' she said. 'I had just had supper and was brushing my hair when a great tiger leapt through the window. At the sight of the beast I fainted clean away and remember nothing more.'

In no time at all her parents were informed of her safety and, since the young pair had fallen in love, they gave their consent to the marriage. Shortly after, the wedding was held and the kidnapped girl and her rescuer began to live in peace and happiness in their humble home.

But that was not the end of the story.

For one day a few years later, the tiger appeared in the yard again; it stood in the far corner, pawing the ground and swinging its long tail slowly from side to side.

That evening, when he came home from the paddy fields, the young man found the tiger lying dead in the corner of the yard. So he buried it in the damp earth that still bore its paw marks.

From that day on his fortunes changed: he soon became one of the wealthiest men in the province, building a big house for his family. Three years after the tiger's death, a persimmon tree suddenly grew upon its grave and every year produced the most delicious fruit.

Still today, the persimmon tree grows and bears fruit within a village in Zangsu Province. I have tasted its fruits myself, which is how I came to hear this story.

The Hare's Liver

A LONG, LONG time ago, the Dragon King of the Eastern Ocean, ruler of the underwater realm, fell sick with a strange disease. The royal physician was summoned and he, in turn, called in the best doctors in the ocean world. They read the royal pulse, tapped the royal cranium, and put their ears to the royal chest.

Then they huddled together in a corner of the bedchamber and muttered amongst themselves. All that could be heard was a mumbling, sighing, and clicking of tongues. After due deliberation, they shuffled towards the royal bed, heads bowed in sorrow.

'Come on, come on, out with it, you fools!' shouted the sick monarch. 'What's the matter with me?'

'Your Royal Highness, you are very sick,' said the royal physician in hushed tones.

'I know that, you idiot,' cried the king. 'It's

your job to cure me. If I die, you all die. Mark my words!'

'Yes, yes, indeed, Sire,' muttered the old sage. 'Yes, indeed . . . It's just that, well . . . there's no cure for you.'

The courtiers standing round the bed all gasped in horror and held their breath.

'No cure, that is, in your underwater realm.'

The courtiers all breathed again.

'For you to regain your health, Your Majesty must eat the fresh, red-raw liver of a land animal, the long-eared hare. Only hare's liver can save Your Majesty's life.'

'Then fetch me the liver without more ado!' wheezed the king, coughing and sneezing into his handkerchief.

'But, Your Majesty,' continued the sage, 'aren't you forgetting that we sea creatures cannot survive on land. We would die before we could catch a hare.'

'Fiddlesticks!' exclaimed the king. 'There is one among you who can survive on land; he shall go.'

The courtiers all glanced about them un-easily. Who was it? Then there came a snuffling noise at the back of the chamber and, as the courtiers made way, an aged turtle slowly ambled forward.

When he reached the royal couch, he said, 'You are right, Sire. I am as much at home on land as in the sea. I will gladly go to fetch you a hare.

But there's just one problem: I've no idea what a hare looks like, I've never set eyes on one in my life.'

At once the Dragon King called for his court artists.

'Now, you dabbling daubers,' he cried, 'paint me a picture of a hare: with long floppy ears, lanky legs, grey fur, twitchy nose, and crossed eyes.'

In no time at all the artists had produced a lifelike portrait of a hare; and this the turtle tucked under his shell before setting off on his quest to cure the ailing king.

First he pushed himself up to the surface of the sea, then he swam and swam until his strength gave out. He floated along with the tide, then paddled some more until, eventually, he spied a sandy shore. As he waded on to the beach, he saw it was a beautiful spring day: gaudy birds and butterflies filled the blue sky; little creatures—crabs and mice, frogs and voles—crossed his path. Yet none of them resembled the picture in his shell.

So he waddled to the top of a grassy knoll and craned his neck in all directions.

Now he could see bigger animals: snakes and foxes, dogs and cats. But they, too, were unlike the picture in his shell.

He slowly climbed an even bigger hill and peered about. All at once, he spotted a grey furry figure down below amidst a clump of clover. It was nibbling the tender green leaves and shoots.

Hurrying along as best he could towards the

long-eared animal, the turtle called out as he drew near, 'Hello there, pardon me, just a second...'

But the turtle's cry startled the nervous hare who hastily hopped away.

Yet hares are as curious as they are nervous. And the moment the turtle turned his back, out from behind a bush leapt the hare and, creeping up on the turtle, tapped on his shell.

'Who are you?' he asked.

The turtle almost jumped out of his shell.

'Oh, you did give me a scare! Why, I've heard so much about you, Mr Hare; I wanted to see you for myself. I'm Turtle, from the Eastern Sea. How do you do?'

'Pleased to meet you, I'm sure,' said the hare politely. 'But what are you doing so far from home?'

The hare, being a vain fellow, was naturally delighted that the turtle had come all this way to meet him; but he was still a mite suspicious.

'Well, apart from coming to meet you, I wanted to see what life's like on land,' the turtle said. 'You see, I've never ventured far on land before. I wanted to discover if it was as beautiful as the land beneath the sea.'

'And is it?' asked the hare.

'You mean to say that you haven't seen the underwater world?' asked the turtle in mock amazement.

'No, I haven't,' admitted the hare.

'Now that's a crying shame,' said the turtle. 'I must say I'm surprised that an animal like you has not seen everything and been everywhere.'

'Well, I've seen all there is to see in the land above the sea,' said the hare. 'But I've never ventured to the bottom of the ocean.'

'Then come with me now,' the turtle said. 'I'll show you wonders you've never dreamed of, sights to make your head swim.'

'No, no, everyone says that we land creatures cannot enter the sea realm.'

'They are right,' said the turtle. 'Entry is forbidden to all but a fortunate few; you are lucky. For I can take you there safely. Just think of all the exciting adventures you will be able to tell your friends about on your return.'

The hare hesitated.

'Well, I suppose that would be something; they would be very envious. Right, I'll go.'

The turtle was delighted that he had tricked the simple hare; and he said, 'Hop on my back and we'll be off.'

The turtle shuffled slowly down to the seashore, with the hare perched on his back, holding tightly to his shell. All along the way he boasted of his adventures on the land.

'Now, hold on tight,' cried the turtle as they reached the margin of the sea.

And he waded through the waves, paddled hard and dived down and down to the bottom of the sea. Finally, they came to the underwater realm. How thrilled the hare was with all he saw: the pink coral reefs, the glittering mother-of-pearl shells, the scuttling crabs, the shimmering shoals of fish.

'You are to have an audience with the Underwater King,' announced the turtle.

The hare could hardly believe his ears. He puffed out his chest, wiggled his ears, and hopped down upon the wet sand.

'Now just wait here for me while I make the arrangements,' said the turtle, shuffling off.

As the hare waited patiently in a large hall of the king's palace, a party of cuttlefish suddenly swam towards him. The hare could hardly contain himself.

'Do you know, I'm to have an audience with the king?' he boasted.

'Yes, yes, we know,' the cuttlefish all replied. 'The king's been expecting you; he's dying to meet you.'

'Well, well,' gasped the hare. 'You mean the king has heard of me?'

'Of course,' said the cuttlefish. 'You are the dearest creature to him in all the world.'

The cuttlefish all tittered.

'What's so funny?' asked the hare.

'Nothing. It's just that the king is a keen admirer of your liver.'

So saying, one of the cuttlefish wrapped a long tentacle round the hare.

'Your good, fresh, life-giving liver,' he repeated.

By now the hare was growing nervous.

'What's my liver got to do with it?' he cried. 'I don't understand.'

'You will soon,' said the cuttlefish. 'Now come with us, we mustn't keep the king waiting.'

They led the poor hare through another great chamber until they came to high pearl-encrusted doors. As the doors parted, the cuttlefish led in the unfortunate hare.

'Your Majesty,' announced the cuttlefish. 'We present to you a hare with fresh, red-raw liver.'

The poor hare's knees were knocking, his pink ears were quivering as he saw the terrifying Dragon King towering over him.

'Welcome to my underwater realm,' growled the Dragon King in a hoarse voice. 'As I may not have much time, I will be brief. You are here for me to eat your liver; it is the only cure for my sickness. Do not grieve. Take it as an honour to save me from an untimely death. I can promise you a decent funeral and a modest monument to your good deed. After all, it is better to die in a good cause than to be struck down by some hunter's arrow or a fox's jaws.'

The hare desperately tried to hide his panic. He bowed low to the Dragon King, then to the courtiers about the royal bed, and to the swordfish guards waiting to cut him down. Finally, he turned to face the king, saying humbly, 'Your Majesty, I am indeed most honoured; and I would gladly give my life to continue your noble reign. Unfortunately, there is a slight problem: I do not have my liver with me . . .'

'What!' roared the king. 'How can you live without your liver? I don't believe you.'

'But it is true, Sire,' the hare continued. 'You see, my liver has special powers to heal the sick; so it is always in great demand. Therefore, I'm always having to hide it. Since I use it mostly at night, I keep it hidden in the daytime. If only the turtle had told me of your need, I would have willingly brought it here.'

The king was puzzled. Looking round at his courtiers, he muttered, 'Surely no one can take their liver in and out as they please?'

'Quite right, Sire, quite right,' they all chorused.

The hare quickly pressed home his point.

'See here, Your Majesty, take a close look at my mouth. You can see my upper lip is split, cleft in two: that's so that I can take out my liver easily.'

The bedchamber was silent. All necks craned to view the hare's cleft upper lip.

Before anyone could say a word, the hare continued, 'Now, I'll just pop home and get my liver, if it please Your Majesty; turtle can show the way to ensure my swift return. But we'd better hurry before Your Majesty . . . er . . . you know what I mean . . .'

And he bowed his head in sorrow.

'Turtle,' exclaimed the king, 'take the hare back quickly to fetch his liver and have him back here as soon as possible.'

The turtle and the hare departed at once. When at last the turtle waded on to the sandy beach, the hare hopped from his back and gave a dance for joy. He chuckled until he thought his liver really would pop out of his mouth.

'Despite your ripe old age,' he said to the turtle, 'you believed all that nonsense about me taking my liver in and out. Ha, ha, ha! I fooled you good and proper.'

And he hopped away, still laughing at his trickery.

The poor turtle wept in anguish as he thought of the dying king. He knew he would never catch another hare now, not after that rascal had warned them all.

All of a sudden, from out of nowhere, there appeared a god with a long white beard and flowing robes. Coming up to the turtle, he said in a deep voice, 'I admire your loyalty to your king. Perhaps I can help. Here, take these ginseng roots. They will cure his sickness and bring him back to health.'

The turtle thanked the divine spirit and hurried back to the underwater palace, delivering the roots to the Dragon King. When His Majesty had eaten the ginseng he recovered his health in next to no time; he made the turtle the highest-ranking minister at his court.

Ever since, the Korean people have used ginseng roots to cure the sick and keep the healthy fit.

How Cat Saved the
Magic Amber

IN A SMALL village beside the river there lived an old innkeeper named Ku. He lived alone except for his cat and dog who were his constant companions. The cat kept the storeroom free of rats; the dog guarded the inn.

Ku sold only one kind of wine, but it was very good. Folk would come from far and near to try his wine, and travellers would often ask for a jug to take with them.

But there was something strange about Ku's wine. No matter how much he sold he never seemed to run out. His neighbours never saw any wine being delivered, and they knew he did not make his own. So where did he obtain his wine? That was a secret Ku shared only with his cat and dog.

And the secret was this. One cold, rainy night, when he was just locking the inn door, he heard a knock. There stood a stranger.

'Can you spare me a cup of wine?' the stranger asked. 'I'm chilled to the bone.'

'Do come in,' said Ku. 'My wine jug is all but empty, but you are welcome to what's left.'

Ku emptied the contents of the jug into a cup for the stranger. The man, however, poured a little of it back into the jug, then drained his cup thirstily.

'You have been most kind,' he said to Ku. 'I want you to have this as a token of my appreciation. Keep it in your wine jug and you'll never run dry.'

So saying he handed Ku a lump of amber.

Ku turned the amber over in his hand and then, with a laugh, dropped it into his wine jug and forgot all about it. Feeling hungry, he ate a few pieces of dried fish and eyed the jug.

'Maybe there's a sip of wine left in it,' he thought, picking up the jug.

What a shock he had . . . The jug was full to the brim.

He poured himself out a full mug of wine and took a sip. It was the sweetest, most excellent wine he had ever tasted. He drained the mug and poured another. Yet the wine level in the jug remained the same.

'How wonderful,' he laughed. 'I'm the luckiest innkeeper in the world.'

From that day on Ku had an endless supply of wine and kept the merriest tavern in the district.

But then one day something terrible happened. As Ku picked up his jug to pour wine for a customer, he found it empty. He shook and shook it, but to no avail. The jug was bone dry.

'I must have poured the amber into someone's cup or jug,' he wailed. 'Now what am I to do?'

The cat and dog became just as miserable, sharing their master's grief; they sniffed around the inn trying to find the amber.

'I'm sure I could find it if I could pick up the scent,' the cat told the dog.

'Then let's go in search,' replied the dog. 'We must make our master happy again.'

Off they went, determined to find the amber. They prowled from shop to shop, house to house throughout the village. Nothing. Then they decided to search houses on the other side of the river; but they had to wait for winter when the water froze to get across.

When winter came they crossed the river ice every day in search of the missing amber. Nothing. Finally, as spring was coming and the ice was beginning to thaw, the cat caught the scent of amber: it was coming from a wooden box on top of a chest in an old house. How were they to get at it? If the cat pushed the box off the chest, someone would hear; in any case, the box was too big for the dog to carry in his mouth.

'I know,' said the cat, 'let's ask the rats to help

us. They can gnaw a hole in the box and fetch the amber out for us.'

'But the rats are your enemy,' said the dog. 'Surely they would not help us.'

'If I promised not to chase them for ten years,' suggested the cat, 'they might do me a favour.'

The rats agreed to the bargain. It took several days for them to gnaw a hole large enough for a small rat to enter the box and fetch the amber in its teeth. Thereupon, the cat took the amber in her mouth and ran off together with the dog down to the river.

'Oh no,' cried the cat when they reached the water's edge. 'The ice has melted. Now how will we get across? You know I cannot swim.'

'I'll carry you on my back while you keep the amber safely in your mouth,' said the dog.

So the cat climbed on to the dog's back and the dog began swimming across the river. Presently, he asked, 'Is the amber safe?'

With the amber in her mouth, the cat could not reply. Not long after, the dog asked again, 'Is the amber safe?'

The cat was becoming cross with the stupid dog. But she could say nothing with the amber in her mouth.

When they reached the middle of the river, the dog asked again, 'Is the amber safe? Is the amber safe?'

Again and again he put the same question,

until as they neared the bank he shouted, 'Why don't you answer? Is the amber safe?'

The cat was so angry by now that she shouted back, 'Of course it's safe . . .'

And the amber fell into the water.

The cat and dog were so furious with each other that they set to arguing and fighting. Finally, the cat had to climb a tree to escape from the angry dog. When the dog had skulked off home, the cat climbed down and walked along the riverbank where some men were fishing. All of a sudden, she caught the scent of the amber. It was coming from a fish that one of the fishermen had just pulled in. In a flash, the cat grabbed it with her teeth and raced away before the fishermen could catch her. She took it home to Ku.

'That's a good cat,' said Ku, when she dropped the fish at his feet. 'That will make a good supper for us.'

When Ku cut open the fish he could scarce believe his eyes. For there inside was his amber. Locking it in a chest, he ran out to buy a jug of wine so that he could re-open his inn. Yet when he returned and opened the chest, he was astonished to find two purses of money instead of one, two jackets instead of one, two combs instead of one. Everything had doubled. Thus Ku learned the secret of the amber: it doubled everything it touched.

Now he grew richer than he had ever

dreamed possible. He made sure that his cat was always well fed, yet he often wondered what had happened to his other four-legged companion. He was not to know that never again would cat and dog live together in harmony. The dog never again killed a rat, but he chased every cat that crossed his path.

Choi Chum-Ji

IN THE TOWN of Jinju there once lived a well-to-do miser by the name of Choi Chum-Ji. His meanness was legendary. He would have nothing on his dining table but boiled rice and soya sauce. Whenever mealtime came, he would run round and round his courtyard before sitting down to eat. Should anyone ask him why he took such vigorous exercise, he would say, 'If you run till it hurts you'll forget all about the taste of food and be content with rice.'

One day while eating his rice, Choi Chum-Ji noticed a fly sitting on the edge of the soya cup and sipping the sauce.

'You cheating insect, steal my sauce would you, I'll kill you for that!' he roared, chasing the hapless fly around the room.

The fly managed to evade him and flew out of the open door with the miser in pursuit, screaming, 'You won't get away with it. I can eat two spoonfuls of rice with a drop of soya sauce; and you would deprive me of that drop of sauce.'

Finally he caught the fly and quickly put it into his mouth; he chewed it several times so as to squeeze all the soya sauce out of its body. Smiling with satisfaction, he went back into the house, having swallowed the dead fly.

Choi's family was ashamed of his meanness, especially his daughter-in-law who was not used to eating rice without meat or fish or vegetables. One day, as a fishmonger was passing the house, she called him to the gate, telling him she wished to buy fish. The fishmonger was most surprised, never having sold fish to the Choi household before. In the meantime, the daughter-in-law kept turning over the fish, trying to select exactly what she needed.

Picking up one fish she would complain that it was not fresh or fit to eat. That made the fishmonger angry.

'My fish are all fresh,' he grumbled. 'They were caught only this morning.'

After a while, she asked, 'How much is this fish?'

'Four *puns*,' came the answer.

'And this, and this?' she continued, turning over each fish in turn.

'This costs two *puns*, this one is one *pun*,' intoned the fishmonger testily.

At last the daughter-in-law chose the biggest

fish and tried to knock down the price to half a *pun*. That made the man angrier still.

'This fish is worth a *nyang* at the very least. I could get seven *puns* for it at market; I certainly won't sell it for half a *pun*.'

'Then you can keep your fish,' she cried. 'I don't want any.'

With that she slammed the gate and went indoors without cleaning the fish scales from her hands. Carefully, she held her hands over a soup pot and had a servant pour water over them, so washing the scales into the pot. Then she made fish soup from the water containing the fish scales.

At mealtime, there was a pot of fish soup standing on the table. Choi Chum-Ji went red in the face when he saw it; he flew into such a rage his voice could be heard all down the street.

'Who asked you to buy fish?' he ranted and raved. 'Who dares to get fish without my permission?'

When he learned that his daughter-in-law was the guilty party he was even more furious. Then she explained the whole story, expecting him to praise her for her thriftiness. After all, she had made fish soup without spending any money.

But the miser was still discontent.

'What a waste,' he cried. 'If you had washed your hands in the well, we could have enjoyed fish soup for months.'

The Sun, the Moon, and the Stars

THERE ONCE lived a woman with her three daughters in a cottage down in the valley. One day, as she was leaving for market, she told her girls, 'Hai-Sun, Dal-Sun, and Byul-Sun, listen well. You must lock the door from the inside until I return. Don't open it to anyone; it could be the tiger come down from the mountain.'

Thereupon, she departed for the town, leaving the three girls alone in the house. Later that day, as darkness was falling, there was a sudden knock—rat-a-tat-tat—at the door. The children were frightened.

'Who is it?' asked Hai-Sun.

'It is your mother,' came a voice. 'Open up, Hai-Sun, Dal-Sun, and Byul-Sun.'

The youngest daughter, Byul-Sun, was so relieved to hear her mother's voice that she went to unlock the door. But the eldest girl, Hai-Sun, was uncertain: was it their mother's voice or not?

So she stopped her sister from opening the door, calling, 'If you are our mother, why is your voice so husky?'

'What do you mean "husky"?' came the voice again. 'If it is, it's because I'm hoarse from crying at market all day long: "Come, buy my vegetables! Come, buy my vegetables!" That's made my voice so husky.'

But Dal-Sun now began to have her doubts.

'If you really are our mother,' she said, 'let us see your eyes through the crack in the door.'

A big, red eye could be seen through the crack. It was certainly not their mother's. It belonged to the tiger who had come to eat the children.

'But why are your eyes so big and red?' cried Byul-Sun. 'Our mother has kind brown eyes.'

'My dear children,' came the tiger's voice, 'my eyes are red because of the red pepper I've brought from market; the wind blew some of it into my eyes.'

Hai-Sun then spoke up, 'If you really are our mother, show us your hands.'

The tiger pushed his two front paws through a crack in the door: they were a black-striped yellow colour and furry.

This made the children even more afraid.

'But our mother's hands are smooth and white,' cried the three girls together. 'Why are yours so yellow and furry?'

'Oh, that's because I stopped to pick some yellow flowers by the wayside,' answered the tiger. 'The thorns tore my skin and the yellow pollen stuck to my hands.'

The three children, being innocent, finally believed the tiger and opened the door. Even now they did not recognize the wicked tiger, for it was wearing their mother's clothes and had her headscarf pulled down low over its head. The tiger had eaten their mother and taken her clothes.

'You look hungry,' said the tiger. 'Just wait a minute and I'll cook you some supper.'

With that the tiger went into the kitchen, trying to make up its mind which child to eat first: should it be Hai-Sun, Dal-Sun, or Byul-Sun?

How scared the children were, however, when they caught sight of the tiger's long tail sticking out from under the skirt. While the tiger was busy in the kitchen, the three girls quickly ran out of the house and climbed the tree in the garden. So when the tiger came out of the kitchen, it found the room empty.

'Children, come and have your supper,' the tiger called. 'I've cooked a tasty meal for you, my darlings.'

All the while it was searching through the house, out in the garden, under the hedgerow and, last of all, down in the well. It was there, in the clear water of the well, that it saw the children's reflection up in the tree.

'Ah, so there you are,' it cried, looking up at the branches of the tree. 'I've been hunting all over for you. Come on down, my dears.'

'No, no, no!' cried the children, trembling with fear.

So the tiger started to climb the tree. But the trunk was too smooth for the tiger's paws to grip and it kept slipping back down.

'Tell me, my darlings,' it said in a whining voice, 'how did you climb this tree?'

'We used sesame oil from the cupboard,' said Hai-Sun. 'We put it on our hands and feet.'

Believing the eldest girl's words, the tiger smeared its paws with sesame oil and tried again. Of course, it kept slipping and sliding and falling to the ground.

'My dear children,' cried the tiger, 'please teach me how to climb. Your mother wants to climb up to be with you.'

Byul-Sun, the youngest sister, could not stop laughing at the tiger's ridiculous antics. She quite forgot the danger they were in and called down, 'If I were you, I'd cut notches in the tree with an axe.'

The moment the tiger heard this, it fetched an axe and began to cut notches in the tree trunk so that it could climb up easily.

Closer and closer the tiger came, its paws nearly touching their feet, its hot breath searing their legs. In their panic, the three sisters called upon the Heavenly Ruler for help.

'Hwan-In, Hwan-In,' they cried. 'The tiger is almost upon us. Please save us. Send down a thick rope to pull us up.'

Immediately a golden rope descended from the skies and the girls clung to it tightly. When they were all safely clutching the rope, it slowly rose beyond the tiger's reach and disappeared into the clouds.

Seeing this, the tiger, too, began to call upon the Heavenly Ruler.

'Hwan-In, Hwan-In,' the tiger cried, 'send me a rope.'

And another rope came down from the skies. This the tiger grabbed and rose into the clouds. However, the rope was too slender for its weight, and on the way up into the clouds it suddenly broke, sending the tiger tumbling down to earth with a great thump. The tiger's body exploded into a thousand pieces and its blood was spattered all over the earth around.

Where the tiger fell was a field of millet and, from that day on, millet stems have always been dark red, stained with tiger's blood.

As for the three daughters, they reached the land beyond the skies and turned into Hai-Sun the Sun, Dal-Sun the Moon, and Byul-Sun the Morning Star. Now they shine upon the whole world, bringing light and hope to all people.

Bride Island

AT DAWN ONE day a young woman was climbing the steep mountain path up to the mist-mantled shrine of the mountain god. In the dim light of early morning she often stumbled over rocks and stumps, but she was determined to reach her goal. She had only been married for a month, but her husband had been struck down by a mysterious disease, and now she was to pray for his health at the shrine.

'Dear Mountain God,' she cried, bowing low, 'please help cure my husband. I will do anything to make him well.'

As she prayed, the morning mist lifted from the valley and smoke curled up from the chimneys of cottages nestling at the foot of the mountain. Beyond the small village lay the blue sea and, far out to sea, were the Seven Mountains—seven islands shrouded in mist and seemingly linked by arms upon each other's shoulders.

She loved her husband dearly. When they had married his illness seemed no more than a chill, yet steadily it grew worse until now he could not leave his bed. She had purchased all kinds of herbs to make him better, selling all her wedding presents and most of her household goods to buy new medicines. But none of them helped. Not discouraged, she prayed each day at daybreak to the mountain god to help her find a cure.

As soon as she saw the chimney smoke, she hurried down the mountain to make some rice soup for her husband. Arriving at the door of her humble cottage, she could hear her husband's groans: it broke her heart to hear him in such pain. If there existed a medicine to cure him she would surely fetch it, no matter how hard the trip might be.

Tears rolled down her cheeks as she stood at the door. Just at that moment an old fortuneteller was passing; when she saw the young wife weeping, she tried to soothe her with a kind word.

'Don't lose heart,' she said. 'Faith can move mountains; your prayers are bound to help your husband recover from his sickness.'

The young woman looked up hopefully.

'If my husband's illness does not get better he will die soon. Granny, if you know of any cure, please tell me; I will do anything to save him.'

She would rather die herself than let her beloved husband pass away. Seeing her eyes shining with love and determination, the old fortuneteller kept silent for a while, then spoke slowly and hesitantly, 'Dear lady, there is a way, but it is far too arduous for a woman to undertake. Indeed, Heaven might punish me even for telling you . . .'

The fortuneteller was reluctant to proceed.

Clutching at her sleeve, the grieving wife begged her to help. And after a while she spoke again, 'You must cross the sea to the Seven Mountains; on the far side of the smallest mountain there is a mysterious yellow plant growing amidst the rocks. They say it can bring even a dead person back to life.'

The wife was overjoyed, thinking it not so difficult to obtain the medicine after all. But she saw fear and anguish in the woman's eyes.

'What is it, Granny?'

'You must know, my dear, that the island is called Devil's Island. No man has ever returned; and they say that a woman would turn into something hideous should she set foot on it.'

'Nevertheless, I will go there to try to save my husband's life,' said the young woman, her eyes shining with hope.

Thanking the fortuneteller, she entered the house to cook breakfast for her sick husband. And she told him of her quest.

'Dear husband, drink this soup, it will do you good. I have left some food for you by your bedside; I am going on a journey and may be late getting back. I've heard there is a plant on the smallest of the Seven Mountains; it can cure your sickness.'

She did not dare tell him of the dangers. Besides, she thought she could be there and back by evening if she took his fishing boat.

Although he tried to stop her going, she tore herself away and set out for the magic island in the small boat. The island did not look at all forbidding as she approached it: it was covered in lush green grass and the same venerable trees that decorated the mainland; there seemed nothing mysterious about the island.

As soon as she reached dry land, she ran quickly in search of the magic plant. She turned up stones and heavy rocks, she searched among the gnarled roots of trees and long reedy grass. Yet nowhere could she find the mysterious yellow plant. She walked all round the island, desperately seeking the medicine. But, as the fortuneteller had said, 'Faith can move mountains', and, as the shadows of twilight were beginning to lengthen, she spotted the plant growing in a crevice between two rocks.

With a cry of joy, she carefully picked the precious plant.

Straightaway there came a hissing sound all about her: 'Sshh, sshhh, ssshhhh . . .' The leaves of the trees tossed and trembled; a sudden gust of wind rattled the stones and rustled the grass; and a menacing hissing broke out. As she turned, she let out a terrifying scream, for all around her were snakes of every size and colour slithering towards her, flicking their tongues at her. The poor girl fainted.

When she recovered the snakes had gone; all was as still as a breathless sea. And the precious yellow plant was still lying beside her. She was beginning to think it was all a dream when she looked down at herself... And she let out a despairing scream once more. For her entire body, from head to toe, had turned into the body of a snake. No arms, no legs, just long, green, scaly coils.

What had she done to deserve this fate? Was she not trying to save her husband's life? But there was no use bewailing her fate if that was the price of the magic herb. Now she had to get the medicine to her husband as soon as possible.

Next morning, fishermen were surprised to see a sea serpent sliding through the waves towards the shore, carrying a yellow herb in its mouth. They watched in fear as the creature reached dry land and crawled towards the village, passing through until it came to a tumbledown cottage on the other side. There it wriggled through the door and disappeared.

The serpent was not to know that the sick man had died during the night while waiting for his wife's return. He had lost all hope when the fortuneteller had told him of his wife's hopeless quest: no one had ever returned alive from Devil's Island. He had succumbed to his disease, unwilling to live without his beloved wife. Early that morning the villagers had buried his body at the foot of the mountain.

The hissing snake dropped the yellow plant beside the empty bed and returned the way it had come, crossing the sea towards the Seven Mountains. And it was never seen again. Yet, as the villagers watched from the shore, they saw an amazing sight.

'Look,' they shouted, 'the island is moving, it is changing shape.'

And indeed, the moment the snake had reached Devil's Island the island took the form of the young bride who had sacrificed herself to save her husband. Then the old fortuneteller told the astounded villagers the story of the poor woman.

'So the snake we saw was really the dead man's bride,' she said. 'She turned into a snake because she went to Devil's Island to help cure her husband, so deeply did she love him. And now the island has taken the form of the grieving bride in memory of her love and sacrifice.'

After that a mysterious sound of weeping could be heard from the island whenever it rained: like the wind rustling in the trees and the waves beating upon the shore. And once a year, on the day when the husband died, a large serpent would cross the sea to take a yellow plant to the abandoned cottage.

The villagers named it Bride Island after the devoted wife.

The Long-Nosed Princess

L ONG AGO there lived an old widow with her three sons. They were neither rich nor poor, and worked hard for their comforts.

One day the widow summoned her sons to her and, with a deep sigh, told them this:

'My dear sons, I am not long for this world. Do not grieve, I've lived a long and happy life. Before I die, however, I want to show you our family treasures.'

Thereupon she reached into an old wooden chest and brought out a small bundle wrapped in a silk cloth. As she unwrapped it, she murmured softly, as if wishing no one else to hear, 'These three treasures have been in our family for many generations; they are so precious you must not show or tell anyone about them. Heed my words.'

First she revealed a glass marble which she placed before her on the floor. Beside it she put a bamboo flute and a ragged old coat. She gave a tired smile of pride as she gazed at her treasures.

The brothers exchanged doubting glances.

'Mother,' said the eldest, 'these are but common objects.'

'Quite worthless,' said the second brother.

'Old junk,' said the youngest.

Their mother smiled to herself.

'You will see what you will see,' she said mysteriously.

And taking the marble in her hand she rolled it slowly across the floorboards. To the amazement of the doubting brothers, it left a trail of golden coins upon the floor.

'What a marvel,' cried the eldest son.

'We'll be wealthy,' said the second.

'But who is to have it?' asked the third.

'Not so fast,' their mother exclaimed with a laugh. 'The marble is for you, my eldest son. You must use it only for the good of you all and only in your hour of need. It is not to be used to make you rich.'

'As you say, Mother,' said the eldest son ruefully.

'The flute goes to my middle son,' she continued. 'It is a magic flute: when you play it a regiment of soldiers will appear and stand ready for your orders.'

And she handed the flute to her second son.

To the third she gave the ragged coat.

'Whenever you put on this coat,' she explained, 'you will become invisible.'

She instructed them to take good care of the treasures and to pass them on to their children and their children's children. Her last piece of advice was this:

'Remember, do not show them to anyone, for if you do, they will want them for themselves and do anything to get their hands on them.'

Not long after, the widow died. Her body was barely cold before the two eldest brothers started to boast about their mother's gifts. Although the youngest constantly reminded them of their mother's warning, they ignored him, bragging even more.

News of the magic gifts soon reached the ears of a certain selfish princess who decided to have the treasures for herself. So she sent a message to the eldest brother to come to the palace and show the court his wonderful marble. The brother was greatly honoured by the invitation and, concealing the marble inside his coat, he set off to visit the princess.

Once at the palace, he was welcomed in person by the princess, entertained by musicians and dancers and served the most tasty dishes. It was not long before the wine and the princess's flattery went to his head, and he took the magic marble from inside his coat to show her its wonderful properties.

He rolled the marble across the shining parquet floor and, lo and behold, it left a trail of glittering golden coins in its wake.

'How wonderful,' gasped the princess. 'Let me see it again.'

He was happy to oblige. Again and again he rolled it over the floor to the obvious delight of the princess. All of a sudden, however, she jumped up and snatched the marble from the floor, hiding it inside her dress. With a triumphant laugh, she had the poor man dragged off to the dungeons.

Next day she despatched another messenger with an invitation to the second brother. And he too was flattered to receive an invitation to the palace; he left without more ado, tucking the magic flute inside his jacket.

Just like his brother, he received a royal welcome: music, dancing, sweetmeats. Most of all he was enraptured by the attention paid him by the princess. At last, when he had consumed more than his share of wine, he told her, 'I have something, Your Highness, that will play sweeter music than that of your musicians.'

'Oh, do show it to me,' she begged.

At once he took out his flute and went to play it. But before it reached his lips, the princess gave a little cry of delight:

'Oh, how marvellous. Do let me try it first.'

Without thinking, he handed her the flute, smiling gaily at having won her interest. She put the flute to her lips and blew into it. In an instant a whole regiment of soldiers appeared, standing to attention and awaiting orders.

With a laugh, the princess shouted, 'Take this fool off to the dungeons and lock him up.'

So the second brother shared the first brother's fate.

As the days went by, the youngest brother wondered what had happened to his two brothers. At last he decided to go to the palace to discover for himself. He had heard tell that the princess was both cunning and greedy: she could well have robbed his brothers of their treasures.

On arriving at the palace walls, he put on the magic coat and slipped through the gates unnoticed. Making his way through the palace in search of his brothers, he came by chance upon the princess in her chamber playing with the magic marble and counting up the golden coins. The sound of her greedy laughter made him so angry he carelessly knocked over a table.

The princess jumped, startled, swiftly hiding the marble and flute underneath the carpet on which she was sitting.

'Guards, guards,' she called, 'search the room. There's an intruder here.'

But no one was found. The princess thought it must have been the wind; so she continued playing with the marble and piling up the coins. This time the brother tried to retrieve the flute from under the carpet. But, despite his caution, his hand brushed against the princess's leg and she cried out again, 'Guards, guards. There is someone here, I know it.'

As the guards rushed round and round in circles, searching for the invisible man, the youngest brother slipped out of the chamber and into the palace gardens. There he sat down beneath an apple tree bearing juicy red and yellow fruit.

Feeling hungry, he picked a large red apple and took a big bite. While he was eating the apple, a strange thing happened: his nose began to grow until it was as long as his arm.

'Oh dear, oh dear,' he cried. 'What am I to do?'

As he was lamenting his fate, he carelessly picked up a yellow apple and took a bite of that. With each bite his nose became shorter and shorter until it had regained its normal size.

Realizing his new powers, he began to laugh.

'I'll teach that greedy princess a lesson she'll remember for the rest of her days.'

He picked some red apples, placed them in a basket lying upon the ground nearby and removed his magic coat. Then he took the apples to a spot beneath the princess's window and started to shout, 'Apples, apples, juicy apples. Who'll buy my apples?'

It was not long before the greedy princess poked her head out of the window and, eager to eat the red juicy fruit, sent a servant down to buy them all. Handing over his basket to the servant, the youngest brother then slipped on the magic coat and made his way as silently as he could to the princess's chamber. He was just in time to see her nose grow to the size of her arm.

'Oh my goodness!' she cried. 'Look at my nose. What has happened to it?'

Her maids and guards came running in at her horrified cries. But they could scarce contain their laughter at the funny sight: there was the greedy princess with a nose as long as a broomstick. Amidst the commotion, the invisible brother crept into the room, took the marble and flute from under the carpet and quickly made his escape. When he reached the palace yard, he quickly blew on the flute and summoned up the regiment of soldiers. Together they searched the palace and soon found his brothers hidden in the dungeons.

After that all three brothers never breathed a word about their treasures again; and they passed them on to their children with the same warning as that given by their mother. As for the greedy princess, she was stuck with the broomstick nose for the rest of her gloomy days. It was to remind her of the price she paid for being greedy.

The Magic Club

THERE WERE once two brothers, one rich and greedy, the other poor and kind. Although it was the duty of the elder son to care for his aged parents, he had sent them to live with his poor brother. And that hard-working soul would go each day up the mountain slopes to cut firewood which he would sell to feed his parents.

One day, as the poor brother was cutting wood, something dropped on his head from the tree above him. It was a big hazelnut.

'I'll give this to Father,' he thought to himself, putting the nut into his pocket.

A few moments later another nut hit him on the head.

'I'll keep this one for Mother,' he said, putting it into his pocket.

Shortly after, a pair of big hazelnuts fell with a 'plop-plop' upon his head, and the kind brother at once thought of his elder brother and his wife.

'This pair of nuts will make a nice present and perhaps bring them luck,' he thought.

And he continued with his work, cutting wood and storing it in bundles beneath the trees. His woodcutting had taken him far into the hills and by now it was growing dark; what is more, a big storm was brewing, with large raindrops already splashing all around. He was relieved to see an old wooden house amid the trees farther up the mountain.

There being no one around, he entered the abandoned house to shelter from the rain. It was not long before he was fast asleep upon the floor. He woke up in total darkness to the sound of heavy footsteps approaching the house. Peering out through a crack in the door, he saw several odd-looking figures.

'It could be a band of thieves,' he thought to himself. 'I'd better hide lest they kill me for finding their lair.'

Scrambling up on to a beam below the roof, he watched anxiously as the footsteps came closer and the door flew open. He could hear the babble of strange voices in the room below as he sat trembling upon the wooden beam. Looking down, he saw a sight that almost made him fall off the beam.

They were not human beings at all, but *tokkaebis*, devils with horns sticking out of their heads. He had heard tell of the *tokkaebis*: they were constantly playing the most fiendish tricks on humans, leading travellers astray in the forest, snagging fishermen's nets, sweeping women's washing down the stream, and sometimes even stealing the souls of innocent children.

Now they were squatting on the floor, telling tales of that day's adventures.

'I spent the entire day teasing a naughty boy, pulling his hair, tripping him up, knocking him into a ditch to muddy his clothes.'

'And I kept tugging on a fisherman's line to make him think he'd caught a fish.'

'As for me, I blew soot down a chimney all over the floor the mistress had just scrubbed.'

But the fourth devil was gloomy.

'I've been searching everywhere for a dutiful son; it's so hard to find one these days.'

After chatting for a while, one of the *tokkaebis* shouted, 'I'm famished. Let's have some food and wine.'

And taking a club from his belt he struck the floorboards with it, crying, 'Come out, rice and wine, come out, rice and wine!'

At once a great pot of cooked rice and a cask of wine appeared from nowhere, standing in the middle of the floor. That was followed by fish, eggs, cake, and fruit.

When they had eaten their fill, the devils decided to count their fortune. Once again, one of them took out his club and struck the floor with it, shouting, 'Come out, silver, come out, gold!'

Straightaway, piles of gold and silver coins appeared from nowhere—to the great delight of the watching devils.

The poor man watching from his perch below the roof was amazed at all this wealth. But he was also made hungry by the sight and smell of the food. Feeling in his pocket he took out a hazelnut and tried to crack it with his teeth, as softly as he could. Alas! The crack echoed round the rafters and was heard by the devils below.

'What was that?' cried a *tokkaebi*.

'It must be the roof falling in from the storm!' cried another.

'Quick, let's get out of here before we're all buried,' screamed a third.

In a panic they all rushed from the house and through the forest.

The poor boy was too scared to come down from his beam and waited until the first rays of dawn showed through the door before venturing down.

Looking round to make sure the *tokkaebis* had gone, he then sat down upon the floor to eat the remains of the feast. To his surprise he also found a magic club they had left behind in their haste. Being curious, he struck the floor with it, calling, 'Come out, silver, come out, gold.'

Lo and behold! A pile of gold and silver coins appeared from nowhere. Gathering them up, he hurried home with the magic club under his arm and the coins jingling in his pocket. With the new-found wealth he bought a large piece of land for his parents and himself. Whenever he needed food or clothes, he only had to strike the floor with the magic club and say, 'Come out, meat or fish or rice; come out, fine clothes; come out, silver or gold.'

And as much as he needed appeared in an instant.

It was not long before the elder brother became jealous of his brother's wealth and decided to test out the story for himself. So he set out for the selfsame hazelnut tree, shook it, filled his pockets with nuts and made for the abandoned house. There he waited upon the beam until the devils appeared in the middle of the night.

In came the *tokkaebis*, told their tales, ate their fill, and thumped the floor with their magic clubs, making gold and silver coins appear. At the sight of such glittering wealth, the elder brother could not contain himself. Putting several nuts into his mouth, he cracked them with his teeth, muttering, 'That'll scare you devils and make you run away.'

'Did you hear that?' asked a devil.

'Yes, we did,' the others chorused.

'It must be that fellow who tricked us last

time and escaped with my club,' said one of them angrily. 'Come on, let's find the villain.'

It was not long before they spotted the elder brother and dragged him down. He screamed and squealed, but the devils just laughed as they thumped and thwacked him. All night long they tormented him: tickling him under the arms, tickling the soles of his feet. Finally, they struck his neck and his feet with their magic clubs, shrieking, 'Come out, neck, come out, feet.'

When they had finished with him he looked like a giant squirming eel.

At the crack of dawn, the devils made off into the forest, cackling and chortling. As for the greedy brother, he somehow made his way home, having to endure the stares and sniggers of the villagers. When his brother heard of the misfortune, however, he at once came to his aid. With one tap of the magic club upon his brother's neck and feet, he soon made them short again.

And from that time on the greedy brother was greedy no more. He had learned his lesson.

Three Dead Wives

ONE DAY, long ago, the emperor summoned his three foremost ministers: the Prime Minister, the Minister for Home Affairs, and the Minister for Education.

'Tell me, gentlemen, why are you each unmarried?'

The emperor, having married more than once, was suspicious of any minister who did not have a wife. So each now related his story. First came the Prime Minister.

'When I was a young student I married my childhood sweetheart. Being a student I was very poor, so my wife did sewing and darning for our neighbours to earn enough money to keep us both. One day when I returned from college I noticed my wife eating something which she hastily concealed as I came in. Naturally, I asked her what she was eating, since I myself was very hungry. Surely she would not deceive me? I flew into a temper when she denied hiding food, but finally she took out a lump of clay and showed it to me, explaining that her throat was so dry she licked the clay so as to be able to continue with her work; after all, her work earned us food. I was so ashamed I apologized on my knees and never suspected her again.

'A few years later I had passed my examinations and gained the post of Governor of Zezu, the largest of the islands in the Korean Straits. I set out to take up this post along with my wife and my servants. The crossing was stormy and since we were in danger of sinking, the captain, who was a very superstitious man, like all mariners, claimed that the gods were angry with us for having a woman on board. Although I argued with him, the word reached my wife's ears and she flung herself overboard without hesitation. Straightaway, the wind dropped, the waves grew still, the storm abated, and we reached the island without further mishap. My wife had sacrificed herself to save us and enable me to take up my post on Zezu. It is through her that I quickly rose to my present post. I could never marry again and be unfaithful to the memory of such a virtuous woman.'

The emperor was moved by the story of the Prime Minister's wife and praised his reasons for not remarrying. He turned to the Minister for Home Affairs.

'I also took a wife when I was young. Soon

after, I suffered a grave injustice: some scoundrels made up a false charge against me and I was sent into exile. When I took leave of my wife, I told her I would not return until an egg could stand upright upon another egg—meaning I would never return. She, however, took me at my word and did all she could, in every moment of her waking life, to make one egg stand upright upon another.

'Five years passed and one night a royal counsellor happened to be passing my old house when he heard a woman's cry. Peering in at the window he was surprised to see my wife jumping up and down in delight, her eyes fixed on two eggs upon the floor. Opening the door, he asked her why she was so overjoyed; and she told him she had just stood one egg upright upon another. That meant her husband would soon return. Being puzzled by her words, the counsellor listened to her story: how her husband had been falsely charged and unjustly exiled. He was moved by her devotion and promised to look into the case; finding that what she said was true he went straight to the late emperor and gained my release.

'Sadly, that is not the end of the story. When I returned home, my wife was waiting at the gate, overcome with excitement. But the years of waiting had taken their toll, and the moment she set eyes on me she fell down in a dead faint and never recovered. So you see, Your Majesty, I could never repay the debt I owe my dead wife and I would never remarry.'

The emperor praised the minister for his devotion and turned to the third minister. The Minister for Education then told his tale.

'When I married at a tender age I was ignorant of women. After the wedding ceremony at my bride's parents' house, I waited in our nuptial room for my young wife to be brought to me. It was a moment I dreaded, not knowing what to do; I sat in the corner with my back to the door. Her mother led her in and left us all alone. I was too shy even to turn and look at her, let alone speak.

'We sat in silence for a while until I felt a tug at my sleeve. Appalled at such forwardness, unbecoming of an innocent bride, I sprang up and rushed from the house back to my parents' home. After that I devoted myself to my studies: I went away to a temple on a mountain-top, remained there for several years until I passed all my examinations. And I was appointed the Chief Magistrate of Namyang in Gyong-Gi Province.

'I set out for Namyang from Suwon, and on the way I passed through a large village. My coach halted in the centre of the village and I was entreated to say a prayer at an old, abandoned house there. I was told that many years before, the daughter of the house had been wed to a young man who had run away on their wedding night.

She still lay upon the bed in her wedding dress, her eyes staring into space.

'Willingly I agreed and was approaching the house when I suddenly recalled that this was the very same village, the very same house where I had been married all those years before. The house was now deserted, but I made my way to the room where I found my bride still lying, quite dead; yet her body was as fresh as if it were only yesterday that we had wed. Her eyes stared at me in accusation and resentment. That look haunted me so much I began to wonder about the events of that fateful night. So I sat down in the same corner as I had on my wedding night, my arms on the wooden table before me. All of a sudden, I felt someone tugging at my sleeve. I quickly glanced round, but my bride was still lying there as dead as a doornail. Looking down, my heart froze: a nail sticking out of the table was catching on my sleeve; whenever I moved, it pulled at the sleeve.

'To my despair, I now realized my mistake of all those years before. How could I have blamed her, completely innocent of the action I had condemned? I tiptoed miserably over to the sleeping beauty and kissed her for the first time, upon the forehead. The moment I did so her body decayed to dust before my eyes.

'She was a shy, innocent, and very rare beauty; I had lost her through my stupidity, through lack of trust. I have never forgiven myself. But the lesson I learned helped me to master my emotions and so reach the post I hold today. For that I owe much to my dead bride. Therefore, Your Majesty, I could never marry again and betray the trust of one so pure and innocent.'

The emperor sighed.

'Gentlemen,' he said, 'you have all three suffered tragic love, and yet it is that experience which has made you the men you are today. Your three dead wives are really responsible for your positions and we owe them all a debt of gratitude.'

The Four Mighty Brothers

LONG AGO an old man found a baby boy lying abandoned outside his house. Having no son of his own, the man took the baby in and cared for it. Yet the baby grew not by the day but by the hour. Instead of drinking milk, it ate cooked rice. When the boy was a month old, he asked his father to make him a pack for his back in which he would bring down wood from the mountains.

So his father made him one of straw.

'This is not strong enough,' the boy declared.

So his father made him one of wood.

'This is not strong enough either,' he said.

So his father had a blacksmith make one of iron.

This time the boy was content and went off to the mountains with the iron pack upon his back. Later that day the old man was surprised to see a mountain of wood moving towards him. Seeing his son underneath it, however, he realized it was actually a load of wood that his son was carrying on his back.

With some of the wood the son built a large house; and he brought great stone blocks from the quarry for gateposts. So strong was he that everyone called him 'Iron Back'.

One day he set off for a journey across the mountains. As he was resting on a hillside he noticed a tall tree acting strangely in a neighbouring field: it kept falling over and rising up again. His curiosity aroused, he went down to the field and discovered a young man sleeping beneath the tree, snoring loudly. As he breathed out his breath was so strong that it blew down the tree; yet when he breathed in the tree was sucked upright again. Iron Back roused the sleeping lad and suggested to him that they become brothers and go about the world. Snorer readily agreed. But before setting off, they had a wrestling match to see who should be the senior brother: Snorer was victorious.

As they were walking about the world, they came to a mighty mountain. Imagine their surprise to see the mountain abruptly crumble and a level field appear in its place. As they came closer, they noticed a young man with a long iron rake levelling the soil. He too was invited to be their sworn brother. Eldest or youngest? This time they tested their strength by Snorer and Iron Back sitting on the rake and asking Raker to move it.

Since he could not, they made him the youngest brother. And off they went together.

In the passing of time they came to a river and were surprised to find it swollen and surging past them in yellow torrents. This they found odd because there had been no rain recently. So they followed the river upstream until they came upon a young man urinating into the valley. It was evidently he who was responsible for the gushing torrent. To make sure, they took him by the neck and shook him hard: at once a giant waterfall almost drowned them. Waterfall became their eldest brother.

Now the four sworn brothers, Iron Back, Snorer, Raker, and Waterfall, set out to travel the world together.

They wandered all day long up hill and down dale until at nightfall they came to a big house. Knocking boldly at the door, they asked if they might stay the night and have a bite to eat. The old woman who opened the door readily invited them in and treated them to venison, as much as they could eat. As they were having their meal, however, they were alarmed to hear the door being locked from the outside.

Since they could not go out, they pretended to lie down and go to sleep; in the middle of the night, they heard voices outside.

'Mother, I can smell human flesh,' came one voice.

'How many have you caught?' came another.

'They smell delicious,' came a third voice.

'Let's light the fire and roast them now,' came a fourth.

Listening to the voices, the four brothers realized that the old woman and her four sons were not humans at all, but tigers who had taken human form. Soon they felt the stone floor growing hot. The tigers had evidently lit a fire underneath the house to cook the four brothers. But Snorer was unperturbed; he blew hard upon the stone floor to keep it cool, so that when the tigers opened the door they were amazed to find the four brothers unharmed.

Next morning the old woman proposed a wood-cutting contest between her four sons and the four brothers. The sworn brothers were to go and cut pine-trees on the mountainside, while her sons would pile the logs up by the house. It was agreed.

The four sworn brothers went out and tore pine trees up by the roots, sending them rolling down the slopes to the four tiger brothers below. It was soon clear that there were more logs coming down than the tigers could pile up. So the old woman shouted that it was time to change over. This time the tiger brothers went up the mountain and the sworn brothers began piling up the logs. But Iron Back and his brothers worked so fast that they had to take a nap while waiting for more logs to arrive. Afraid that her sons were losing the contest, the sly old woman set fire to the pile of logs so as to burn the brothers standing on top of it.

This time it was Waterfall who came to the rescue: he urinated upon the logs to put out the fire; not only did he put out the fire, he caused a great flood that soon engulfed the tigers up to their necks. Once in the water, the old woman and her four sons changed back into their tiger form and showed only their heads and forepaws above the flood.

From their place of safety upon the logs, the brothers ignored the tigers' shouts for help and called on Snorer to blow cold breath upon the water, turning it to ice. In no time at all the tigers were frozen stiff. Then Iron Back skated over the ice and snapped off the tiger heads and feet, scattering them all over the ice. Finally, Raker took his iron rake and smashed the thick ice into pieces, hurling it far and wide and restoring the earth to its former state. No trace remained of the great flood.

As for the four mighty brothers, they went on their way across the world, doing good deeds whenever they were called upon.

Adventures of the Three Sons

L ONG AGO, there was an old man who lay
dying. Summoning his three sons to his
bedside, he bade them farewell with these
words:

'I am a poor man with nothing much to leave
you. None the less, your inheritance may one day
bring you good fortune. To my eldest son I leave
my millstone; to my middle son I leave my
bamboo walking stick and gourd bowl; and to
my youngest I bequeath my drum. Bless you,
my sons.'

With these words, the breath departed from
his body. Soon after, the brothers set out into the
world, bearing their father's gifts; they shortly
came to the parting of the ways and agreed to meet
ten years hence at that very spot. Then they parted,
one turning to the left, one going straight ahead,
and one turning right.

The eldest son walked along the left hand

path with the millstone on his back until dusk
made the path too hard to see. Afraid of sleeping
upon the ground in case a wild animal or robber
stole up on him in the night, he climbed a tall tree,
taking his millstone with him, and settled in the
branches to sleep.

In the depths of the dark night, however, he
was awoken by the sounds of two men arguing on
the ground below the tree. It was two robbers
disputing the division of their spoils; suddenly the
two men were surprised to feel heavy rain upon
their heads and hear muffled thunder right above
them. It was actually the eldest brother urinating
from the tree and grinding his millstone above
their heads. The robbers took to their heels and
fled to safety.

When they were far out of sight, the eldest
son climbed down from the tree and found a
sackful of coins and jewels. Early next morning he
set out happily for the next village where he
decided to make his home. With his gold coins he
bought a large house and married the most
beautiful girl in the village.

Meanwhile, the second son had taken the
middle path and as twilight fell found himself
walking past a graveyard outside a village. Since
he could not see the way ahead, he decided to
make a bed for himself upon a burial mound. In
the depths of the dark night he was startled to hear
heavy footsteps coming straight towards him.

Shrinking back behind the mound, he heard a voice addressing him, 'Come on, corpse, wake up and have some fun.'

It was a *tokkaebi*, one of those devils who go abroad in darkness to torment human souls.

'Gladly,' answered the second son.

But the devil was wary at hearing a human voice.

'Your voice doesn't sound dead,' it said. 'Are you playing tricks on me?'

'Oh no,' cried the second son, trying to make his voice sound hollow. 'I've been dead these past ten years.'

'Let me feel your skull then,' said the *tokkaebi*.

Holding out his father's gourd bowl, he wheezed, 'Here, feel it; it's a dead skull all right.'

The devil rubbed its hand over the rough gourd and sounded satisfied. 'Good,' it said, 'your skull's all rough and hairless. Let's just feel your arm to make sure.'

The second son poked out the bamboo walking stick, muttering, 'You're hard to please, aren't you. Here, feel my bones.'

Feeling the walking stick, the devil was now content.

'Ah, a skinny skeleton, you must be long dead. Right, let's go. We're going to steal the spirit of a wealthy man's daughter tonight.'

Off they went together and soon came to the gate of a large tiled house. In a husky whisper, the devil told the second son, 'You wait here, corpse. I'll pop in and snatch the girl's spirit while she's asleep.'

With that it was gone. A few minutes later it was back clutching something in its hand.

'Hey, have you got something we can keep the soul in?' it asked. 'We don't want to lose it.'

'I've a purse on me,' said the second son. 'Put it in there and I'll pull the strings tight so that it can't escape.'

That done, the two of them made their way back to the graveyard; by now it was growing light and they could hear a cock crow in the village. At that the *tokkaebi* bade the son farewell, 'I must hurry. Look after the soul for me till tomorrow. I'll see you then.'

The moment the devil vanished, the second son rushed back to the big house carrying the purse with the living spirit inside. Hearing wailing from within the house he discovered that the wealthy man's only daughter had died suddenly during the night, leaving her parents overcome with grief. No doctor could do anything to save the girl or even identify the cause of death. At that the second son went straight to the mourning parents and told them, 'I may be able to bring your daughter back to life.'

The father readily agreed to accept help if only it would restore his dearest daughter to life.

'But there is one condition,' said the second

son. 'No one else must come or look into the room while I'm at work.'

That agreed, the father took him to the dead daughter's room and left him all alone. The second son locked the door and pasted rice paper over the windows and all the cracks in the walls and door; then he placed a screen around the bed. That done, he took the squirming purse from inside his jacket and put it right underneath the dead girl's nostrils. Loosening the purse-strings with his free hand he let the spirit out: with a whoosh and a whistle it flew straight into her nostrils.

After a moment she opened her eyes, perfectly healthy again. So delighted were the girl's parents that they immediately offered their daughter in marriage to the second son. The young pair were soon wed and lived happily thereafter in the large house.

In the meantime, the youngest son had taken the path to the right. As he walked along the path through the hills, he beat his father's drum slung round his neck and sang songs to keep his spirits up. All at once, as he rounded a bend, a huge tiger emerged from the trees and started to dance to the music. The terrified young man realized that if he should stop playing the tiger would seize him instantly and eat him up. So he went on playing, walking backwards so as to face the tiger all the time.

Before long, the youngest son came to a

village where all the villagers came out to see the strange sight. They imagined that the tiger was tame and the master had trained it to dance. So enthralled were they that they showered the young man with gifts in payment for the amusement.

The youngest son realized that he could turn misfortune into fortune and he led the tiger all the way to the capital city, beating his drum and singing. The emperor himself came out to see the odd pair, inviting the man and his tiger to the palace to perform. Once there, the emperor's youngest daughter fell in love with him, and the emperor agreed to their marriage.

So the youngest son became a royal prince and lived happily in the royal palace. As for the tiger, it soon grew to prefer life at the palace as a royal pet to its former existence in the forest.

When ten years had passed, the three brothers returned to the spot from where they had started out on their adventures. After recounting their tales and rejoicing in each other's luck, they went together to the graves of their parents, thanking them in prayer for the good fortune that their father's gifts had brought.

The Centipede Girl

THERE WAS once a man living in Seoul who was so poor he could not feed his family. In despair he decided one day to put an end to his worthless life. So he went down to the River Han and walked along the high bank until he came to a tall cliff; there he stopped, took a deep breath and threw himself over the top.

He never imagined he could survive such a plunge on to the strand below. Yet not long after, he opened his eyes to see the beautiful features of a young woman leaning over him. She had seen him fall as she was washing clothes in the river.

'You are very fortunate to have fallen into deep water,' she said. 'I managed to pull you out on to this sand bank. How on earth did you come to fall over the cliff?'

He recounted his unhappy life and his attempt to end it all.

'Oh, how dreadful,' she said, her hand covering her mouth in horror. 'But you are still young and may yet find fortune. You had better come home with me now and rest before you travel on.'

Thereupon she helped him to his feet and, with one arm round his shoulders, she led him along the riverbank until they came to a big brick-built house with a tiled roof standing alone in the river valley. The lovely woman attended to his every need, feeding him tasty sweetmeats and rubbing balm into all his cuts and bruises. He stayed on for days, then weeks, and soon came to fall deeply in love with the mistress of the house. He cast his family right out of mind. In any case, he reasoned, they will surely think he was dead, for he had often talked of throwing himself into the river.

So the weeks merged into months and he continued his carefree life with the mysterious young woman. Now and then, however, his thoughts turned to the poor wife and children he had abandoned back in Seoul. The sensitive mistress of the house guessed his thoughts and one day told him, 'I know you wish to see your family again; I cannot keep you here against your will. But remember, if you leave me now you will forget me and not return.'

'Oh no,' he answered truthfully. 'How could I ever forget you? Trust me: I shall come back soon.'

'Well, if you do return,' she said, 'mark these

words. Pay no heed to anyone who tries to deter you. Ignore them, come straight back and I shall be here waiting for you.'

He did not understand the note of anxiety in her voice. But he set off back to his family, walking along the banks of the River Han; suddenly, as he reached the suburbs of the city, he was astonished to behold a splendid new abode upon the site where his old home had been. As he drew near he even saw his own name inscribed upon the gate.

He knocked rather timidly on the gate and was overjoyed to see his son appear to open it. The boy gazed fondly at his father with tears of joy streaming down his cheeks.

'Mother, Mother,' he cried. 'It's Father. He has come home.'

She came rushing into the courtyard, dressed in the most elegant clothes.

Suspicious thoughts passed through his mind.

'Who built this big house?' he said sternly. 'And who bought you those beautiful clothes?'

'Why, you did,' replied his wife in surprise. 'Do you not remember sending me money every day? Surely it was you who sent us all those marvellous gifts?'

It began to dawn on him: the mysterious woman must have provided everything; no one else could have helped his family. So he swiftly changed the subject, said nothing of his attempt to take his own life or of the mysterious woman he had been living with. He had to pretend that he himself was the benefactor.

He was content to be back with his wife and children; yet as the months passed he could not forget the woman who had saved him. Thoughts of her constantly troubled his mind until he could bear it no longer. Once more he left his family and made steps for the big house in the valley.

His path happened to pass a clump of trees standing above the river. As he drew near he was surprised to hear a hoarse voice calling him by name; it sounded exactly like his long–departed grandfather.

'Dear Grandson,' echoed the voice from a hollow tree, 'I am the spirit of your grandfather. Heed my words: turn back and return to your family. You must not go to that woman in the valley; if you do she will destroy you. She isn't a woman at all, but an evil centipede.'

The man was confused. It certainly sounded like his grandfather's voice. Yet surely what it said could not be true?

'Grandfather, if it really be you,' he said falteringly, 'I do not fear death, for I have known it too intimately. But I will not be distracted from my purpose, nor persuaded that she is evil after all she has done for my family.'

Back at him came the hollow voice.

'Since you are determined to go on, so be it. But, dear Grandson, I tell you this for your own

good. There is only one way for you to avoid
death: take good strong tobacco, chew it and
retain the juice in your mouth. The moment you
set eyes on the evil centipede woman, spit the
black juice into her face. Otherwise you will not
break the spell she has cast over you.'

The voice had sown the seeds of doubt in his
mind. So he called in at the market on his way and
bought some strong tobacco; this he put in his
mouth and began to chew as he went towards the
house in the valley. When he arrived at the house,
he crept quietly round to the back and peeped in
through a crack in the door. To his horror he did
indeed see the tail of a huge centipede and, with
sinking heart, chewed all the more fiercely on the
tobacco.

He knocked loudly on the door which, after a
delay, opened to reveal the mysterious woman,
just as lovely as ever. She invited him in and was
obviously glad to see him. He spoke no word to
her—how could he with his mouth full of the
poisonous tobacco juice? Noticing his clenched
teeth and the suspicion in his eyes, she guessed that
he had not heeded her warning. And she grew pale
with anxiety. What would he do?

As he entered the house he was torn between
his love for her and the dire fate forecast for him by
the voice in the tree. Remembering what he had
spied through the back door, however, he made
up his mind that he had to carry out the voice's

orders. So he pursed his lips and was about to spit the juice into her face when she burst into tears. His heart melted as he gazed into her beautiful tear-stained face and, as her head was bowed, he quickly spat out the tobacco juice through the open window.

She breathed a deep sigh of relief and smiled up at him through her tears.

'Thank you for sparing me,' she murmured. 'Let me now confess the truth. The voice you heard in the hollow tree was not that of your grandfather; it was the evil serpent that lives in the tree. He was once a lackey in the palace of my father, the Heavenly Ruler; one day he stole a kiss from me for which we both were punished. He was condemned to live forever in the form of a serpent, while I had to live as a centipede for three years in the world of humans.

'The evil serpent is ever eager to do me harm. Today, however, is the last day of my sentence; tomorrow I return to my father. Had you spat the black juice into my face I would have remained a centipede here on earth for three long years more. Come, let us make the most of our last day together.'

And so they did. Together they dreamed the sweetest of dreams, spoke to each other of the love they shared, and lay fondly in each other's arms until the time came to part.

When he awoke next morning, he was

surprised to find himself lying on a sandbank all alone. There was no sign of the house in the river valley. All that remained were his fond memories of the heavenly maid as he trudged back to his earthly home.